PRAISE FOR
THE TEN PERMISSIONS

"*The Ten Permissions* is the 21st-century playbook we've been waiting for. It's smart, soulful, and wildly relevant."

—**JONAS KOFFLER**, *New York Times* best-selling author of *Hustle*

"In a world where the old scripts for success are unravelling, *The Ten Permissions* offers new language for flourishing in the 21st century. The book is a generous, grounded guide for anyone ready to question the rules they've inherited and begin designing a life on their own terms."

—**SIMONE STOLZOFF**, author of *The Good Enough Job*

"I'm not sure I would be a writer today if Jillian Reilly hadn't helped me give myself permission. Her ideas have changed my life, and they might just change yours."

—**TIM HARFORD**, author of *The Undercover Economist*

"*The Ten Permissions* is a bold and counterintuitive guide to thriving in uncertain times. Jillian Reilly challenges us to let go of outdated beliefs and embrace a fluid future with curiosity and courage. Her insights are provocative, actionable, and deeply human. This book aligns with the spirit of my podcast *Imaginize.World*—helping people shape the future before it shapes them. You won't finish it unchanged."

—**JANE MCCONNELL**, host of the *Imaginize.World* podcast; author of *The Gig Mindset Advantage*; researcher, Future2043

"In *The Ten Permissions*, Jillian guides readers on a powerful, uplifting shift in how we live—unlocking agency, hope, and a brighter future in the process. Give yourself permission to read this book!"

—**APRIL RINNE**, author of *Flux*

THE 10 PERMISSIONS

REDEFINING THE RULES OF ADULTING IN THE 21ST CENTURY

THE 10 PERMISSIONS

JILLIAN REILLY

WONDERWELL

Published by Wonderwell Press
Austin, Texas
www.gbgpress.com

Distributed by Greenleaf Book Group

For ordering information or special discounts for bulk purchases, please contact Greenleaf Book Group at PO Box 91869, Austin, TX 78709, 512.891.6100.

Design and composition by Greenleaf Book Group and Mimi Bark
Cover design by Greenleaf Book Group and Mimi Bark

Publisher's Cataloging-in-Publication data is available.

Print ISBN: 978-1-963827-29-3

eBook ISBN: 978-1-963827-30-9

To offset the number of trees consumed in the printing of our books, Greenleaf donates a portion of the proceeds from each printing to the Arbor Day Foundation. Greenleaf Book Group has replaced over 50,000 trees since 2007.

Printed in the United States of America on acid-free paper

25 26 27 28 29 30 31 32 10 9 8 7 6 5 4 3 2 1

First Edition

For Luke and Aidan.

Never stop listening to your inner DJ.

CONTENTS

THE TEN PERMISSIONS

1. Be willful.
2. Go astray.
3. Take it outside.
4. Experiment.
5. Feel your way.
6. Forget about the future.
7. Think small.
8. Travel light.
9. Look for trouble.
10. Make believe.

DEAR READER

You are imprinted with a story about who you're supposed to be and how you should behave.

It's OK; we all are.

We all carry a set of internalized injunctions and permissions that shape who we become: the nature and course of our lives, the choices we allow ourselves to make, and the ones we see as off-limits. We each operate by a set of rules. We all carry with us an internal story.

Some of that story is conscious and explicit. Much of it is unspoken and unconscious—a set of directions you follow without even being aware you are headed toward a specific destination. Directions that are decades old, passed on through generations. Baked into your DNA.

Parts of that internal story likely don't serve you. Maybe they never have. The directions take you to places you don't really want to go while bypassing so many beautiful options along the way. Those story parts aren't about you, and they're not a product of this moment.

This world is calling out for new stories, *now* stories. We desperately need them, and you do too if you're going to make use and sense of all the options available to you in this 21st-century moment. But that means getting explicit about the story you're carrying with you, how it's stopping you or slowing you down, what direction it's setting, and whether that's where or how you want to go. It means getting explicit about your own story.

You're not broken, not deviant, not deficient for wanting to write a story that works for you and for this world. You don't need fixing. You need permission.

You're allowed to let go of the story you didn't write so you can write your own story. But you must grant yourself permission to begin writing.

Yours,
Jillian

A PERMISSION SLIP

These *Ten Permissions* are all about designing a life fit for this crazy world. For the rest of this book, you'll be writing yourself permission slips to do just that.

Before you begin writing your own slips, here's one slip I'm writing for you because accepting this permission will amplify every permission that comes after.

I'm granting you permission to be optimistic.

There's currency to cynicism right now. People are working harder and saving less. Humans are about to be replaced by robots. Politics is broken, and everything's melting. You'll read that story every time you check your phone because fear and pessimism rule and "hopeful" feels like just another name for "clueless." Choosing optimism today is *radical.* Believing in a different and better future is borderline revolutionary when the prevailing narrative is bleak and cynical.

I won't accept that cynical narrative as the only version of today's world. You shouldn't accept it as the only version of your future. You can't afford to. Because fear and pessimism limit your options by making you question whether you have any good options from which to choose. It makes you believe that last century's options were the only good ones. Fear and pessimism urge you to stay small and safe because small and safe are your best option when you're being knocked around and knocked over.

You deserve to choose the life you want, to choose the way you want to live, however that looks. Only you will know what your version looks like. Designing that life, rather than defaulting to the decades-old options, means allowing yourself to be optimistic. Sunny. Confident. Hopeful. Expansive.

With optimism as your starting point, the *Ten Permissions* in this book will set you loose into this world, not keep you safe from it, so you may design a life that stretches out rather than staying small.

Permission to be optimistic is permission to believe that your best days lie ahead in an expansive life that you can't see or maybe even imagine yet. But you believe in yourself, and in this crazy world, enough to go out and create the life you want.

Permission to be optimistic: granted.

INTRODUCTION

When I told my parents I was going to South Africa, they looked at me like they didn't know me anymore. Maybe they didn't. I quickly learned that when nobody else seems to know you, you're getting to know yourself.

At age twenty-three, I started to write my own story, though I didn't call it that. I didn't have words to describe much back then, but I was starting to make my own choices, choices that were singular to me and sometimes only made sense to me. I went to South Africa on the eve of a historic election, when everybody thought the country might blow up. And anyway, how does going to South Africa help anyone get a good job? It would take a while before my parents would get to know the "me" I was becoming, the "me" I wanted to be.

I was supposed to be setting myself up for a good job. Instead, I was setting out to create a good life, not knowing what that meant but sensing it involved some combination of meaning, purpose, connection, and, yes, maybe even adventure. Which was radical in 1992 Middle America and still is now. It was also confusing and disappointing to people who thought they knew me, people who'd decided who I was "supposed to" be, people who couldn't imagine why I'd want to be anything else. Who'd never expected me to break rules that up to then I'd willingly followed.

I walked out of the good-grades, good-school, good-job story to figure out my version of a good life, and—in doing so—allowed the default good-life story to unravel a little. But only a little. You can play around with the default good-life story—say "no" to parts of it and do other parts later—but your version of a good life is still supposed to be one other people recognize and approve of. You never divorce yourself from cultural expectations and social pressures. You keep tapping your own sense of purpose and meaning to find your own unique way one step at a time, which might feel daunting.

I know how lonely it can feel when the people who love you see you as a stranger. I also know sometimes you've got to become a stranger to others to get to know yourself.

THREE REASONS I'VE WRITTEN THIS BOOK

A lot of people are stuck today between old stories and new, what's always been and what's becoming. I'm familiar with how that feels. I've worked all over the world with people stuck in stories they never wanted but couldn't reframe or reclaim, unable or unwilling to give themselves permission. I've spent my career helping people write their own stories while at the same time intentionally writing my own. Nobody's given me permission to write my story—I had to give it to myself.

It's time for you to confidently step toward the future you want, which I know—from that lifetime of learning—is going to take you giving yourself that same permission.

Reason One:
I know something about writing my own story.

I've lived an extraordinary life mostly—though not exclusively—on my own terms.

I've traveled days and nights on airplanes with broken windows and in buses with drunken drivers. I've sat on faraway beaches always deciding to have one more swim before the sunset and made my way through markets selling grilled meats I couldn't name. I've sat around fires with village chiefs and around tables with warring ethnic neighbors. I've experienced things most people couldn't imagine and wouldn't consider, but it's not the glamour or exoticism of my experiences that have made my life extraordinary. It's the fact that I was willing to choose those experiences, to make my own choices.

Working with people in bruised and beautiful parts of the world helped me realize that so many people don't have choices. They are stuck in place to save their lives, not to protect their stability. Economics, culture, and religion keep them tethered to whatever situation they're born into. For them, being stuck was and is a function of circumstance. Any choices they do have feel too dangerous to make.

Maybe you want your version of a good life. Maybe you have thoughts about your life you're too afraid to say. Maybe you don't know what you want, have feelings you can't turn into words. Maybe you're wrangling with "want" and "should," wrangling with what excites you and what pleases other people.

Here's what I've learned: Making everybody else's choices is the easiest. Making your own is the hardest and most satisfying, a kind of superpower.

Because choices are essential to your individual makeup, acting on them affirms your unique identity regardless of whether or how they work out. You're getting to know yourself, beginning to authorize yourself, one choice at a time.

You learn to:

- figure out what *you* want.
- trust your gut and act on your will.
- deal with discomfort and uncertainty.
- live your life in small steps rather than grand stages.

The sooner you learn to make your own choices, the more expansive your life becomes. If you never learn to make them—if you never feel able—you get stuck.

Reason Two:
I've spent too much time with stuck adults.

When I wasn't exploring the world, I was working with people from every walk of life—from executives to villagers and everyone in between—all of whom felt stuck in lives and stories they didn't want but didn't know how to change.

While each person was a gloriously complicated individual, the people I've worked with did share certain characteristics. They:

- stayed put for too long.
- feared risk and uncertainty.
- let fear make their decisions.
- looked to institutions for their identity.
- relied on other people's directions instead of self-directing.

- didn't intentionally build a set of capabilities and experiences.

Regardless of the scope or scale of the available choices, these individuals didn't feel allowed to choose what they wanted.

Here's what I've learned: Getting unstuck is hard and gets harder with every passing year.

The amount of will required to redirect your midlife is overwhelming, so most people never do it, which leads to frustration and despair, the heartache of unfulfilled promise, the grief of living a life that isn't yours.

I've also learned: Being stuck isn't just about the commitments and assets and responsibilities that come with midlife. You forget how to find your own way—if you ever knew at all.

If you can't make your own choices at twenty, making choices doesn't get easier at forty. In the grand scheme, you've made so few of your own choices that you don't know how to make good choices when you feel ready to redesign or redirect a life you've spent decades creating, which makes sense. The very behaviors that got you stuck will never get you unstuck, and learning new behaviors later in life is hard.

Nurturing your growth and evolution will help you avoid becoming stuck in the first place, though it takes self-permission to make your own choices from as early in adulthood as possible.

Somewhere in the world, probably not even very far from where you're reading this book, there is someone who'd give anything to have your choices, someone who has so little power over their own story. If you're lucky enough to live a life rich in choices—and if you're reading this book, I'm guessing you are—then you're able to honor that wealth by making choices you love.

- Don't behave like you've got two choices when you've got twenty.
- Don't complain about your twenty choices when so many people only have two: stay or go, live or die.

Don't lose sight of what a privilege and honor it is to make your own choices whenever and however you can. My extraordinary life taught me that so many people can't.

Reason Three: I'm a mom to Gen Z boys.

The world's hurtling forward at a dizzying pace, and yet the success story is stuck. We're living in a time of deep disruption, relentless change, and vast choices, almost more than we can comprehend. Yet our old-school success stories cling on tighter than ever. In a world of vast possibilities, there's tremendous pressure to stick to the same set of choices a previous generation made. In our safety-seeking human brains, "good" choices will always be the familiar ones.

I'm watching my two sons find their ways to adulthood and witnessing how choice-making plays out in their lives:

- the still-narrow definitions of "success"
- steering toward the most conservative choices
- flirting with exciting life options before returning to the safest

- emphasis on appearing successful to impress the assembled adults
- performing certainty—pretending to "know" what they want to be or do
- flattening what makes them unique, interesting, interested so they can slide into ready-made, recognizable roles

I'm watching my sons confront that familiar battle between "supposed to" and "want to," a battle I fought myself. What surprises me, though, is that "supposed to" hasn't shifted much since the '90s.

It's 2025, and yet 1995 is still renting space in our conversations with young people. Because we can't make sense of the scope and scale of today's change, many of us want to make it go away. Because we're not familiar with the emerging opportunities, we treat them as threats. Because we don't yet know what we'll need to know, we're still trying to armor up with accounting degrees and a banal but reassuring focus on "business." Because we can't agree on new rules, we keep propping up the old ones.

We can shift our thinking for the 21st century. We can do things differently. I've learned a few things in life that I'm now communicating to my children:

- Learning how to make choices early in life sets you up for later.
- Always make your choices consciously and intentionally.
- You *get* to make different choices today, and you must.

These *Ten Permissions* are for my sons, a way for me to say all the things I want to say to them, to capture everything I want them to feel and believe. These *Ten Permissions* are also for all the people I've worked with who've eyed a better life for themselves and then looked away, who somehow didn't feel allowed to design the life they wanted. These *Ten Permissions* set you loose into this world so you don't become (or remain) one of the many people stuck in place, stuck in a coercive story that limits choice or leads to the pernicious belief that the only good choices are the ones that have always been made.

I can see how we're stuck now, stuck between past and future, between the ways we've always lived and the ways we want and need to live now, for this world. Because you don't have to be stuck between yesterday's expectations and today's possibilities, stuck between "get a good job" and "follow your passion."

The world isn't binary, and you have so many more options to choose from than sleepwalking and free-falling. You no longer need to submit your life to secure mediocrity or chase fulfillment on the fringes. You know the old binaries are false dichotomies now because this world, the 21st-century world, doesn't require you to trade satisfaction for security.

How much do you trust yourself? How bold or intentional are you willing to be in seeking satisfaction versus tiptoeing toward things you want, testing how safe it is?

You have a chance, right now, to do things with your life that your grandparents would have found unthinkable, to become things in your life that your parents might have deemed unimaginable. You're allowed to do and be and experience so much! But you'll need permission to take advantage of your options and opportunities, your *own* permissions.

And these *Ten Permissions* will help.

WHAT TO EXPECT FROM THESE *TEN PERMISSIONS*

Imagine if you were unafraid of letting go of the old and familiar and embracing whatever's waiting for you, unafraid to see the chaotic world as your greatest opportunity to create the life you want, and maybe even the world we all want. Imagine treating today's disruption as a feature, not a flaw.

This book is about millions of individual permission slips, but it's more than that—so much more. This book is about social permission to change the bigger stories holding us back, not just rejecting the status quo but collectively imagining a better future, how we live and what we create.

We need a new approach to adulting in the 21st century, but we don't know what it looks like and whether we're allowed to do it in the first place.

I offer you ten direct and specific ways to turn that stuck-in-the-past success story on its head, ten ways you can consciously reimagine your success story and be neither afraid nor reluctant to:

- foster your growth and evolution.
- design a life path that works for you.
- unlock the capabilities most useful to you.
- frame success in terms that make sense to you.
- work with a mindset that facilitates your uniqueness.

These *Ten Permissions* allow you to update your approach to adult life for the chaotic abundance of the 21st century. They show you how to think intentionally about making new choices as an adult in a rapidly changing world and in a way that's practically radical, daring you to think about your life differently while keeping your feet firmly on the ground.

The Ten Permissions

Be willful: Own your authority to design your life, not by attaching yourself to a single entity, institution, or role for protection, but by trusting that you can navigate the chaotic marketplace of the working world.

Go astray: Accept that a linear life may not be in your best interest, that it may limit your choices, even hide the depth and breadth of your options from you.

Take it outside: Go beyond the known and familiar, beyond the auspices of the routine and everyday life, outside your front door with an explorer's mindset.

Experiment: Examine your life through observation and curiosity, ask questions, and place small bets on yourself.

Feel your way: Allow intuition, your powerful gut instincts, to lead you through decision-making processes as you discover what truly lights you up and allows you to flourish.

Forget about the future: The future is amorphous, opaque in its distance. Rather than thinking in years, allow yourself the space and presence to think in days.

Think small: Strategic and tactical step-by-step execution toward your big and unknowable goals, taking the smallest, most sustainable steps.

Travel light: The past had you focused on accumulation over experience, stuff over philosophy, and bills over values. There's no shame in discarding the notion that having lots of stuff is better than having lots of freedom, room to roam.

Look for trouble: Creating a life you love means getting comfortable with discomfort in pursuit of your growth and evolution as a changemaker in today's dynamic world, which may lead you to great contributions.

Make believe: In the digital 21st century, your creativity, your humanness, is what you need most to thrive. Embrace innovation to generate your new life and be your whole self.

See these *Ten Permissions* as a way of updating your adult operating system for the 21st century. That is what's required—a systems update, a new way of operating. What worked in the stable predictability of the 20th century no longer does. This world doesn't care for old logic and rules—it doesn't reward yesterday's approaches and strategies. This world is calling you to shift your approach and show up differently, which means giving yourself permission to loosen your grip on the old stories holding you back.

Together, we'll create self-permissions to allow and accept and applaud a range of adult life stories much better suited to this moment.

	FROM		TO
PERMISSION 1	Compliant	P	Willful
PERMISSION 2	Linear	E	Curvy
PERMISSION 3	Narrow	R	Expansive
PERMISSION 4	Probable	M	Experimental
PERMISSION 5	Cognitive	I	Embodied
PERMISSION 6	Future outcomes	S	Current options
PERMISSION 7	Deductive	S	Inductive
PERMISSION 8	Accumulative	I	Adaptive
PERMISSION 9	Isolated	O	Engaged
PERMISSION 10	Execute	N	Create

Together, we'll foster the fortitude to ditch some of the anxiety, anger, and fear—the shame—so many of us feel, shame that holds us back.

We are not obliged to stay quiet or do it, each of us, by ourselves. Instead, we may intentionally—and yes, even boldly—design lives that work for us and, in the process, start to design a world that works for everyone.

We must imagine. Experiment. Try. Fail. Get lost. Create. Dream.

We *get* to.

And it all starts with permission.

PART 1

THE PERMISSION PARADIGM

FROM SEEKING PERMISSION TO SELF-PERMISSION

I know, I know: self-permission? You spent your whole childhood asking others for permission, and now you need to spend your adult life granting it to yourself?

Achieving success early in life encourages us all to become compliant people-pleasers, but now more than ever, thriving adults must claim their own authority and autonomy.

In a disruptive world overwhelming you with options and opportunities, you must shift from seeking permission to granting self-permission.

NO LONGER GOOD BOYS AND GIRLS

We all wanted to be good boys and girls, which meant seeking approval and asking for permission. Permission slips! Your parents' permission! Like little passports into the world of your wants.

Permission for what you wanted to do: Please may I leave the table?

For what you wanted to express: May I say something?

To meet your visceral needs: May I go to the bathroom?

To do anything extracurricular, extra fun, extraordinary: Will you sign my permission slip?

You spent your youth navigating authority and desire—what you want to do and what you're allowed to do—being rewarded for not only playing by the rules but never questioning them. Young people are raised to defer to authority and fit into systems because they need boundaries and structure, need to learn how to exist within communities, and need to develop the abilities to self-manage and self-regulate. You needed permission to do what you wanted most. You were rewarded for "supposed to" and needed permission for "want to."

Biological and social imperatives create cultures of permission, which see most people entering adulthood guided by three anchoring beliefs or behaviors:

- deference to authority
- compliance with rules
- pursuit of extrinsic rewards—good grades, academic honors

The Permission Paradigm is the imprinted belief that we need permission to act on our wants, which served us as children but holds us back in adulthood. The imprinted Permission Paradigm is latent. It lurks. It's a stealthy part of our operating systems. Though largely unconscious, the imprint goes something like this:

- Acting on your wants requires permission.
- Asking for permission makes you a good person.
- You'll get into trouble if you don't get permission.
- Your goodness is marked by receiving recognition.

You may not know how much you're self-limiting, staying small, or playing it safe because the good boy or girl in you is programmed to avoid anything that looks off-limits. So you tune out your wants, dismiss them as dangerous. You're so used to living by someone else's rules that you cannot fathom making your own. At a certain point in adult life, you've got to get real about the rules you choose to follow, about making your own rules—helping society rewrite them at large.

MAKING SPACE FOR MORE AUTONOMY

The transition into adulthood means nobody's telling you what you're allowed to do or who you're allowed to become, but you've already got a lifetime of learned behavior steering you toward the preapproved choices.

Children are brought up to be permission-seekers, programmed to satisfy the needs of a system to keep them out of trouble. As such, they're not guided toward or being mentored by adults granting their own permissions.

As an adult, you're trying to work out what exactly you're allowed to do or be, but it's far from easy. You're transitioning from a time of responding to outside authority to claiming more of your own. You're making space for more autonomy, which most people don't do intentionally, if ever. You're not used to consciously and intentionally engaging with *your* definitions of right and wrong, good or bad; *your* desires and not someone else's; *your* boundaries. Your rules. So used to seeking green lights from other people, you're not likely used to switching on your own green light. You may not realize your green light exists. You likely don't consciously expect someone else to give you permission to become who you are, to do what you want to do, but you're not used to granting yourself permission.

From Achievement to Authority

It's not that we're failing to prepare young adults to own their authority; it's that we're preoccupied with churning out achievers. We're obsessed with overachievement, always have been, as if all those achievements will protect young adults from the world's chaos. But they won't—they can't. Sadly, the push toward achievement might be doing the opposite.

What wires you for achievement doesn't wire you for your owning your authority. Achieving and overachieving are about satisfying the needs of a system, letting it tell you what "good" looks like, and then being the goodest you can be, all while seeking its approval, which isn't about building authority. Instead, approval-seeking prizes external metrics, measurements, and directives. It's compliance par excellence! Not inherently a bad thing except when it leaves behind young people who view themselves as successful only to enter chaotic adulthood feeling utterly ill-equipped.

The preoccupation with achievement is setting up young adults for failure. We're churning out overachievers who don't have authority and then calling them snowflakes. Yet we haven't owned our part in their lack of preparation for this world.

This world.

Not the world we've come from and are quickly leaving behind.

We're not preparing young adults with the authority to back themselves, to make critical choices, to solve problems; to identify and leverage their unique skills, to think critically in the face of complex challenges; to experiment, and risk, and rise, and fall. We're not preparing young adults to dream.

Shifting the focus from achievement to authority means prizing high agency as much (and probably more) as high grades and rethinking the metrics of a school curriculum that values knowledge more than discovery, reimagining subject matter that's valued and valuable for *this* world. It means decoupling academic capability from life capability and letting go of the reassuring-but-empty idea that good grades mean you'll have a good life, that "success" or "achievement" equals authority.

Those stuck adults I mentioned earlier?

Most of them were "successful" in the eyes of whatever system they were in. But from village to boardroom, they found they were unable to authorize themselves to make the choices *they* wanted. They didn't feel allowed such autonomy by whatever family, corporate, cultural, political, religious, or social system had always dictated their behaviors and choices. When it came time to make their own choices, they didn't know how and were too afraid to try, so blinkered by "supposed to," they had little connection to "want to" or "I can." And there's little in life sadder than a fifty-year-old who still looks to their parents for permission.

You're stuck in a "supposed to" story when:

- you adhere unquestioningly to extrinsic rules that satisfy the needs of a system, be it family, work, culture, or religion, rather than letting your intrinsic needs guide you.
- you sacrifice your own wants to the system that's promising to protect you.
- you chase the system's rewards without a sense of satisfaction, meaning, or reward.

Without self-permission, you may feel paralyzed by:

- indecisiveness.
- overwhelm.
- hesitation.
- confusion.
- anxiety.
- apathy.
- dread.

You're stuck because you've buried your own wants. You've buried your identity beneath everybody else's demands, locked in a battle between what *you* want and what *the system* wants from you.

The result?

- risk avoidance—staying safe at all costs
- closeting—hiding whole parts of yourself
- repression—inability to access your desires

Self-sacrificing, people-pleasing, and striving for external validation—external rewards—mean you may not know the joy of internal rewards. You're always trying to do the right thing, be the good person, make people happy while half wanting or expecting someone else to affirm your very existence. And you're probably exhausted and disempowered in the extreme.

Adult permission-seeking has made for loyal employees and long-suffering spouses, but it hasn't necessarily made for happy humans.

Here's the thing: External permission-seeking no longer creates secure or successful humans either. To be a thriving adult in a wild world, it's time to get intentional about self-permission.

Self-permission is the green light to make your own choices, to consciously claim your autonomy, to deal with the unconscious imprint of the person you think you're supposed to be.

Self-permission is you becoming your own authority figure so you can become the person you want to be. It's about kindling the kind of self-awareness and self-efficacy that allows you to keep growing and evolving and making your best contributions. It may seem selfish, even radical, when you intentionally and routinely give yourself permission. But in doing so, you will become more:

- nimble.
- creative.
- resilient.
- confident.
- persistent.
- risk-ready.
- resourceful.

You'll decide your own way or find your own way. You'll keep going even when you don't know the way. You'll give yourself permission to thrive, and, in your thriving, you'll give this wild world the best person you can be.

I know—oh gosh, do I know—you may think this kind of radical self-permission makes you a demanding taker. But maybe, just maybe, your self-permission makes you a clearer, more focused, and generous contributor out in this world ready to make your best offers and create the greatest value.

TWO REMINDERS AND A REFRAME

Reminder One: You must permit yourself.

We all want other people's approval, and we all enjoy the feeling of getting it. But we don't have to fear *not* getting it. When we've done the work of becoming our own permission givers, we can deal with disapproval.

As a beer-drinking, tax-paying, army-ready adult, nobody can give you the permission you need to take the action you want. Other people can reassure or counsel, support or applaud, but the green light to act lives inside of you and you alone. No boss, parent, or influencer can set you on your path.

You're the only one who can reach the internal permission switch, so you must switch on that green light yourself.

Reminder Two: Self-permission must be intentional and explicit.

I'm a big fan of self-talk. Voice your permissions, whether in whispers, whimpers, even screams. Go all in! Maybe all you say to yourself is "it's OK" or "you're allowed," but even two words spoken out loud and on purpose at the right time will shift your sense of what's possible and acceptable.

So much of self-permission is sitting in conversation with your fears and distinguishing real threats from the imaginary, true danger from discomforts. Ask yourself, "What am I afraid of?" with a little bit of kindness and a whole lot of curiosity. Maybe you'll have an answer; maybe you won't. Doesn't matter. You're starting to engage with the real-life consequences of your choices versus the imagined fears of your internal story.

All along you're in conversation with your inner authority figure about what's possible and allowed, asking: Why? Why not? Who says? Asking yourself the question that raises your awareness of what's at stake for you—what you're protecting, and how fear of rejection, failure, or loss—may steer you toward "want to" over "supposed to." Maybe for the first time, you can answer, "*I* say!" because you accept that, as a beer-drinking, tax-paying adult, you can trust your own authority—to be that authority.

It's OK. You're allowed.

A Reframe: You're strategic, not rebellious.

It still feels strangely rebellious to be intentional with your adult life even as the world requires us to be ever more so. I know it took me years to shrug off feeling like some self-indulgent jerk because I wasn't sitting in traffic or at a desk. That's normal.

Self-permission may feel clumsy at first. Repatterning always feels clumsy and self-conscious, awkward, even reckless. "I say!" might make you feel like a greedy toddler or an out-of-control teen rather than the good adult you imagine you should be.

You're not used to kindling your inner authority, to claiming your choices as your rightful expression of yourself, and you'll likely have more than one wrestling match with your internal good boy or girl.

Hear me out: What if the opposite of a compliant adult isn't a defiant one, but a unique one? What if claiming your own authority isn't "eff you"; it's "yay me"? Self-permission isn't a middle finger at anyone; it's a thumbs up to yourself. It's not about judging the people who came before you or care about you; it's about trusting your own judgment. And it's about being yourself—whatever that looks like—and believing that you really are *allowed* because you've given yourself permission.

Breaking away from the Permission Paradigm doesn't mean throwing away how things have always been done or discarding who you are at core. It's about uncovering that core self and your desires. It's about saying a giant, "yes!" to a life you want rather than a grumpy "no" to a life that doesn't work for you. Breaking away from the Permission Paradigm means deciding things for yourself directly and intentionally—an intentionality that has within it the power to turn today's disruption from a fault to a feature. A chaotic Unraveling to a rich Renaissance.

UNRAVELING FOR THE 21ST-CENTURY RENAISSANCE

This fluid world is issuing you countless permission slips—more than you can maybe manage—and now you've got to write your own. More than any time in human history, you can create the life you want. Still, you may feel like all your adult security blankets have unraveled around you. The world is scary full of potential, but you're hung up on "scary" because the potential doesn't look like your parents' potential.

This is a Renaissance, people!

It's time to step into this world and figure out what it's allowing you to do, who it's allowing you to become, and what you're allowed to create. Allowance takes permission—so much permission—because it feels so precarious. It requires new rules and different choices. And unless you intentionally permit yourself to make different life choices, you'll default to the familiar ones. You'll keep working from old logic when you need new logic.

Fear and pessimism, that old story you carry, will keep you small and self-limiting, will shape your direction and take you back to all the familiar places without you even knowing you've returned to the "supposed to" path.

It's time for new choices. New logic. New stories. New rules. So permit yourself to create a life fit for the future rather than one attached to the past. It's time to adult for the 21st century.

Old Logic in a New World

In the early 2000s, millennials started to worry and wonder, in public, about why adult life felt so hard, about how they were expected to behave, about the choices they were supposed to make, and about whether they'd ever succeed by classic adulting metrics. They felt abandoned, like they were in adulthood alone. And they probably were alone in trying to keep it all together during The Great Unraveling. Thus, the term "adulting" was coined.

Adulting anxiety was the result of people growing up and into a fluid world they expected to look like their parents' world. Here were young people moving into wild unpredictability but still supposed to secure predictably "good" lives by 20th-century standards. The coining of the word was a collective WTF to a world that didn't promise to play by the old rules but also didn't want millennials and others to make their own rules.

Adulting felt impossible and deeply unfair.

Over the past twenty years, adults have become angry and afraid because:

- they don't possess enough assets to buy long-term security.
- they're not gradually accumulating wealth at the rate they expect.
- they don't believe institutions will care for them or that loyalty will serve them.
- they lack stability in their career ascents due to layoffs, poor economies, and global crises.

Adult life feels fractious when it was meant to be seamless. The old adult life strategies aren't paying off in linear progress. Achieving the old version of success, the success many would have us believe matters, seems difficult if not impossible. We joke about the boomer lifestyle but still low-key think the two-kids, big-house, bigger-car success story is the gold standard. We still long for a work–life model that offers the gradual accumulation of wealth and status, and protection from an increasingly chaotic world. Instead, everybody's in it alone, and we're making it up as we go, hustling to patch together lives and livelihoods while waiting for the next pandemic, climate disaster, or AI takeover. Life's so fluid, it can feel like drowning.

We know the old rules are unraveling, but we're not sure we're allowed to make our own, to join others in shaping new social rules.

We still want to trust the formula of the old success story: If you play by the rules, you'll be a good person and have a good life. Maybe, though—twenty-something years into the 21st century—it's time to accept that there *is* no going back, and that's not a bad thing. It's not the fixedness we crave, not really, but the formula for success and security it offered. The formula for the confidence and clarity in our choices that we so desperately want. It's not that we want to go back. We just want to be confident moving forward with some coherent sense of how to create security in a fluid world. Nostalgia comes because we feel scared of the future, because we don't have a strategy for navigating a fluid world.

You do now.

Transitioning from Fixedness to Fluidity

We're living in a deeply disordered world where old systems and ways are crumbling yet new ones aren't entirely visible yet. Every day, there's the sense that nothing—*nothing*—is predictable anymore. Not the weather, not politics, not work. None of them are what you expect them to be, what you think they *should* be.

The velocity and scale of change and the impact of socioeconomic shifts mean we're struggling to make sense of life most days, much less our futures. We're permanently primed for the next upheaval while dire predictions echo in the background. As I write this, people are predicting the demise of the 9-to-5 job. Birth and marriage rates are declining; life spans are increasing. AI is only hinting at its capability and power. The four seasons feel like they no longer exist. Our line of sight is shorter, our sense of control weaker.

"Unprecedented" now feels commonplace. And because we're living through what might be one of the greatest transitions in history, there's a profound fragility as we shift from a state of fixedness, where everything remains constant, to a state of fluidity, where change is the only constant: The Great Unraveling.

The Great Unraveling

- Fixed world: Hierarchical, traditional, periodic innovation, permanence, select information gatekeepers, concentrated authority, aversion to change, adherence to standards. Institutions rule. Formal roles create boundaries. The past predicts the future.
- Fluid world: Flattened hierarchies, liberalized norms, diffuse influence, transience, broad access to information, rapid change. Individuals are paramount. Interpersonal relationships are more important. The present is all you've got, and the future feels unknowable.

In many ways, we've run arms wide open into this fluid world, loving its freedoms and access and choices. *Unraveling has felt like liberation.* As consumers, we're happily ordering our extra-hot, no-foam, single-shot coffees. As creators, we're confidently posting content and opinions, scrolling through countless information sources and streams, valuing wider voices and perspectives. As partners and parents, we're figuring out our approaches rather than feeling like we're stuck in fixed roles. We're reveling in abundant choice, individual liberties, and opportunities to create and be authentic. We're also curled up in the fetal position freaking out.

Security in the *old logic* of the fixed world came by attaching yourself to an institution that promised to protect you in exchange for loyalty and service: a company, marriage, family, or community. *The individual found security in these institutions*, which meant compliance, deference, constancy. You made three big choices—job, spouse, and house—and then held on, gradually gaining status and power. Pick a lane! Stay the course! Play by the rules! And experience the frictionless ascent to social status and security. *Unraveling has left us feeling utterly lost. Our old sources of security are gone, changed beyond recognition.* Who do we trust anymore? What's the right path to follow anymore? What's real or fake? It's hard to know where you stand when the institutions that have knitted our societies together are losing authority all around us. When we don't have faith in the institutions anymore, we need immense faith in ourselves—not easy to accomplish.

The lived experience of all this Unraveling is chronic insecurity and endemic precariousness, the nagging sense that you're either already a failure or bound to become one. That you're doing something wrong—your life is never quite right. Headlines and statistics of twenty- and thirty-something adults suffering from loneliness and anxiety in epidemic proportions back up the sense of collective unraveling.

When governments ignore us, employers fire us, and religious institutions abuse us, who's looking after us? How will we ever feel secure if we're not working a system our whole life? What's the life strategy during The Great Unraveling when "supposed to" is shifting under our feet, and ample choices become overwhelming when choosing career paths, not coffee? How do we navigate the world when we're experiencing the triple whammy of old identities, secure institutions, and agreed-upon rules all unraveling at the same time?

As liberating as it feels to have many potential paths, it's also paralyzing. We don't know which path is right, may not know who we're supposed to be, how we're supposed to behave, as we explore our paths. The pressure on individuals to navigate the fluid world is rife with choices, challenges, and changes. This Great Unraveling has left us feeling untethered to anything known and familiar, anything we think will keep us safe.

Changing authority during The Great Unraveling:

- Weaker external authority means stronger internal authority.
- Diffuse external influence means critical individual choice-making.
- Greater unpredictability means dialed-up personal resourcefulness.

The rules are no longer clear, which is a nightmare for good girls and boys who are dedicated to playing by the rules, taught to defer to external authority and wait for permission to do the right thing. The fluid world feels chaotic if you expect to be held in place by institutions and systems that tell you who you're supposed to be and what you're allowed to do. Directives to do the "right thing" come from everywhere and nowhere. Cue: anxiety, burnout, and depression. Cue: drug addiction and excess. Cue: cultural worry around "adulting." Cue: overwhelm and tuning out. Cue: self-permission to adult for the 21st century.

Writing Your New Success Stories

Imagine moving confidently into your future, accepting that there are so many better success stories suited to this time, stories you're allowed to write and are fully capable of writing. Imagine feeling fully prepared to make bold, decisive life choices.

Writing your new story starts with seeing how the old logic of the fixed world limits you from thriving in this fluid world, making you see all the threats and so few of the opportunities, making you question whether we have any good options at all, whether yesterday's options were the only good options.

We're dealing with the stark reality of impermanence and unpredictability, but in the chaos of the unraveling of the institutions we once thought would keep us safe—by telling us who to be and what we were allowed to do—we get to decide for ourselves. We've *got* to decide for ourselves or risk treading the choice waters. Without self-permission, you may feel lost at sea. With self-permission, the fluid world is your oyster.

The Great Unraveling is a 21st-century Renaissance, a time of boundless opportunity, extreme creativity, and vast potential for innovation. The world isn't breaking; it's more beautiful than ever. And that beauty scares us because it's fast-paced and shape-shifting and offers none of the familiar guarantees of safety. It can't. We're used to outsourcing security and may not feel up to the task, though fostering security offers limitless individual opportunity. We're scared of the 21st-century Renaissance because it makes security an inside job, an individual job. Make no mistake: The security you crave sits inside you.

Is that not what you wanted to hear?

Or is it the permission slip you've been longing to grab and run with?

Your adult life strategy is no longer to find the "right" degree, job, partner, or role and hold onto it for protection. Security isn't a company or a role; it's *you.* Security is your ability to adapt and evolve and intentionally navigate constant change. While that may scare you, it also has the potential to set parts of you free.

The *new logic* of the fluid world prizes flexibility, learning, and creativity. It rewards adaptability and nimbleness. Today's logic tells you to be ready to find new ways of navigating life in a turbulent world. So it's time to start working with this new reality rather than fighting it; it's time to come alive to its possibilities rather than fretting over its failings. Reframe what's possible and what's desirable even if it makes you feel greedy, rebellious, or weird. Because it will feel weird. Life, the world, feels weird right now.

But then, maybe one of the great legacies of the fixed world is that being "normal" isn't all it's cracked up to be.

Old logic: Find institutions that will protect you for life.

New logic: Spend your life nurturing the capability to be your best protection.

Permission to Be Abnormal

Prepare to hush and shush your inner good boy or girl because "normal" is all they were ever groomed to be. Normal kept them out of trouble, and the most ambitious form of normal got them gold stars and grins from the assembled adults. Now, though, the concept of normal feels outdated.

The reality of this fluid world is that feeling abnormal is becoming the norm. Changing norms make everything feel abnormal, and intentionally shifting norms *requires* you to allow yourself to feel abnormal. Is it normal to go to college? Own a home by age thirty? To have kids? Three choices considered the norm only a few decades ago, now completely up for grabs.

Really, nobody can agree on what is normal anymore. So why in the world would you let an ideal of "normal" keep you small and hooked on "supposed to"? Why would you allow your adaptation to this world to be framed and judged as rebellion from the rules of a previous world? Prepare yourself to live weirdly and give yourself permission to feel odd. You get to. And in the fluid world, you've got to.

The old logic told you to sacrifice uniqueness for security—do what everybody else does and become the most familiar version of yourself—to buy success. To bury any wants that weren't like everyone else's, to stifle any questions that poked holes in normal. But you don't have to think chasing normal is your best life strategy. You don't have to worry that feeling weird is a sign that you're making the wrong choices or are on the wrong path. You get to be weird today because nobody's holding you to fifty-year-old rules except yourself.

I know, I know. Someone might not approve. But that someone's opinion need not make your decisions for you.

And guess what? You must get used to feeling weird if you're going to take advantage of the possibilities this fluid world provides, if you're going to let this Great Unraveling unravel what keeps you stuck in place, if you're going to flip your personal Unraveling to your 21st-century Renaissance.

To change, you need permission. To live amidst nonstop change, you need to embed permission into your operating system and routinely authorize yourself to make choices that suit you and serve this moment even when they feel weird because chances are they will. Your best choices may not be the choices everyone else has made or the ones they want you to make.

Each of us gets to work out our own "normal" now; we've *got* to because the new logic might be counterintuitive to the old logic. The new logic isn't weird. It's just a product of today rather than yesterday.

Many of these old-logic/new-logic conversations turn quickly to morality or politics. The question of familiar or unique choices and identities can easily become heated because it's often seen as a judgment of other people's choices rather than an affirmation of your own.

I don't see it that way. Instead, I see the new logic as adapting to a fluid world—to the Unraveling—where we all feel a little more untethered for better or for worse, where keeping our heads down only means we get lost.

Of course, our choices will change. Of course, we'll have fewer kids, if we have them at all, too afraid of having dependents. Of course, we'll "job hop" because we know damn well no company will keep us safe. Of course, we'll speak up more because we know that silence isn't a strategy.

So many of the choices fueling culture or intergenerational wars are just adaptations to a fluid world that put pressure on individuals to navigate fluidity during The Great Unraveling.

We know we're in it alone. We must find our own way. We get to. It's time to do it intentionally and boldly.

SAY HELLO TO YOUR INNER EXPLORER.

This fluid world needs you to find your own way through it making your own choices as you go. It's giving you permission to discover what's possible when you create your own path no matter how weird it feels. You'll need all the permissions you can muster to trust that you're allowed a unique path and have the agency to go find it.

Old logic: Choose from a selection of life options.

New logic: Create your own options.

Follow the leader. Follow the rules. Follow the path.

I see it happening with my boys: the way we look around for who or what we're supposed to become, hoping to recognize ourselves in familiar ways forward. Like trying on suits to find one that fits, we expect to slip into ready-made roles and show up for the rest of our lives looking uniform and familiar. Which used to work in a fixed world where the ways forward were mostly clear and straight and familiar, and your job was to keep looking straight ahead and stay on the path until you got pushed off at retirement.

The success formulas of the fixed world offered if–then guarantees: If I get an accounting degree, then I will have a stable career path. This wasn't the formula of entrepreneurs, innovators, or creators. It was the formula for bosses and workers, titles, and career tracks. You weren't in control of your identity or in charge of your path. You gave that power away to an institution in exchange for protection. In the fixed world, you placed a bet on a company or profession. In a fluid world, it's time to bet on yourself.

Fluid situations don't offer straight paths, predictability, or guarantees. There aren't any signs in the sea. You get to explore different ways to find your way, which is shocking if you expect a marked path, a detailed map, or even just signs to tell you where to turn and how far to go. That shock might be why millennials felt (and may still feel) so shortchanged: They expected to walk the same smooth paths boomers walked only to find those paths torn up and leading to dead ends. They were at sea, drowning.

Shifting from following-the-way to finding-your-own-way is tricky and requires different thinking about moving through adult life in today's world of uncharted territory. So much I-don't-know and figure-it-out drive the fear that generates the possibilities.

- **Following the way:** Straight, narrow, singular; chasing extrinsic desires and rewards; avoiding change. You find your direction from the outside world by following outdated rules and markers.
- **Finding your own way:** Loopy, broad, divergent; internally driving your own change. You find your direction by getting to know and following your gut, by continually exploring changing conditions and adapting to thrive in it.

You're shifting from extrinsic (outer) to intrinsic (inner) guides, shifting from what *they* want to what *you* want. Trusting that you know your own way and can continually find your own way through unfamiliar territory so you can pivot, persist, prepare for change, and effect change means seizing and using your internal authority.

You're giving yourself permission all the time to make choices based on changing wants, needs, and circumstances. You accept a certain transience to your choices and circumstances. You no longer expect predictable outcomes and stable contexts. You're alive and alert to your surroundings and possibilities and what they can teach you. Your work isn't looking forward and staying the course; it's getting ready to change course not to survive but to grow.

Growth is the inherent offer of this Renaissance, the chance to grow and shine as individuals rather than stay fixed in place to prop up institutions. Growth is also where greedy feelings come from: *Who am I to think I can grow and shine when my good-boy or -girl training told me to keep quiet and do my work and satisfy my external requirements?* The old-logic strategy was not to grow our own things but to help companies grow things. The new-logic strategy says we get to grow our own lives now in the service of ourselves and not a company, which can feel bold and reckless and greedy to a lot of people still imprinted with the idea that it's not what they're here to do, that investment in ourselves is only for the few, the artists, the wealthy, the exceptional.

There's audacity in exploring what's possible rather than executing what's known, but being audacious is how we flip the Unraveling to the Renaissance.

The pinnacle adult in that world was the "executive" who executed the plan and followed the straightest line possible to the next major goal or achievement, the one who thrived in a world of deferential rewards-seeking because they knew exactly how to work their way up the hierarchal ladder. The Unraveling has made that kind of executing feel impossible, and following in a fluid world makes you dizzy when you don't know what next month looks like, much less next year.

The thriving 21st-century adult is less executive and more explorer, less cruise control and more rally car. It may sound daunting, but you're perfectly equipped to explore. The old logic said you didn't need to explore, even discouraged you from exploring new ways forward, told you exploration was dangerous. Not anymore. It's time to unleash your inner explorer and switch on the green light that is your agency.

Explorers = High-Agency Humans

Agency is a wonky word with a simple definition: the ability to make intentional choices and act on them. Seizing your agency, though, when you're not used to exercising it, is hard.

Most of us have a hard time tapping into intrinsic choices because we've been conditioned to respond and conform to external forces, to look around for familiar choices rather than listen in to the ones that make sense to us. But looking around doesn't work well anymore. Not when there are a thousand directions and just as many people telling you which direction is right. Not when a fluid world requires trusting your intrinsic drivers to find your way.

Your way may or may not look like everyone else's, but you're authoring your own choices, writing your own script. In the world of vast choice and volatile change, agency—choice-making—is a kind of superpower. The Unraveling creates space to discover, not gaps to fall into. The unfamiliar feels like an opportunity. By firing up your choice-making engine, you set yourself up to find your way through the fluidity. Unraveling becomes Renaissance.

Yesterday's executives were mostly top-notch followers rather than rugged finders. Agency was kryptonite to traditional, hierarchical cultures. It was inconvenient when compliance and conformity were key, where you looked to be told who you were and what you were allowed to do. Your parents and grandparents didn't need high agency in their world.

But that's not your world, is it?

The fixed world resented high-agency humans, but the fluid world rewards agency and maintaining a belief in your power to progress, to find your way through uncertain environments one choice at a time. A belief in your power to make choices is the first step in finding your own way because you authorize yourself to act without outside direction or permission.

You don't wait for conditions to be perfect or for everything to be clear.

You act, consciously and intentionally, even in small steps.

Because that's often the only way forward.

Agency in action looks like:

- initiating rather than waiting.
- intending rather than accepting.
- anticipating rather than reacting.
- risking rather than playing it safe.
- improvising rather than retreating.

Lack of agency looks like:

- sluggishness and hesitancy to act or make decisions.
- spending your life in waiting: Waiting to get pushed out. Waiting for the perfect conditions. Waiting for more information. For the right time. For clear instructions. For praise.

In the absence of high agency, inertia easily takes over. And inertia in a fluid world isn't sitting still; it's staying feverishly in motion until you get washed away.

Inertia is victimhood, seeing yourself as subject to the world rather than being the subject of your own life story. It's an inability to influence or progress. The doom-and-gloom story casts you as a victim in a world that won't look after you, subjecting you to its changes.

Firing up your agency is the antidote to victimhood, turning "Can I?" into "I can!" and "They won't let me" into "I'll let myself." Having high agency means you focus your attention on individual choices rather than circumstances because you're dialed into what your best choices—your only choices—are, what progress looks like even if it's the tiniest step. You're owning your control, which is critical in the fluid world.

The Unraveling feels like we're being tossed around. The sea is storming, and yes, we are drowning. We can all feel so desperately subject to circumstances beyond our control, whether in the world, the office, or the community. Agency brings your attention back to choice, to action. It doesn't promise a happy ending. It simply reminds you of next steps.

You already know that in certain cases, you might not have a lot of choices or power. I've worked with many people who don't. If your only choices lead to danger, then they are not good choices. But for many of us—most?—it's not danger we fear; it's discomfort.

In a fluid world, focusing on circumstances can feel paralyzing, but focusing on choices may show the way forward. That's agency in action, asserting your control over your choices, your story, your path; asserting your power to design the life you want and not the one you think you're supposed to have. While many don't or won't trust their own power and permission to design their lives, you must.

You get to.

Make your good life work.

You're living in a world where you not only get to design your life; you've *got* to design your life out loud and on purpose! If this sounds excessively intentional, remember you're in a fluid world with a thousand different choices to make and no agreed rules to follow. Designing your life is how you go from patching it all together to setting a path forward.

Design is the antidote to inertia, the antidote to doing what's always been done and doing the same thing until circumstance says you can't anymore. Design responds to two core questions that every adult needs to ask themselves, not only when they're setting out or stuck but repeatedly as they adapt and grow:

1. What kind of life do I want?
2. How do I create it?

Simple questions, right? But how many people allow themselves to ask them, much less act on them?

Few.

Few own the authority and agency to drive their choices rather than have their choices dictated. Instead, they default to already-trodden paths, unsure how or afraid to walk their own. Default is an unconscious operating mode marked by the absence of agency or intentional choice. Defaulting to the old logic often means the life you get is one you don't want because it doesn't work well for you.

Permission to design is about putting yourself in a mindset of making intentional choices, routine updates and adaptations, and committing to continued relevance and applicability. Committing to your own rapid evolution alongside the world's.

As part of design, you get intentional and bold about:

- **mindset:** your attitude and expectations.
- **metrics:** how you measure progress and satisfaction.

- **definitions:** what you mean by security, success, and wealth.
- **capabilities:** what you know and what you are prepared to learn and do.

Will you write all this down, sketch out your life with pen and paper? Maybe!

The way many people keep journals and diaries, you might keep a design or sketchbook of your life where you track your updates and evolutions. Some design sketches might be explicit and detailed. For others, sketching is internal and about heightening awareness of these factors, dialing up the intentionality, sparking agency by reminding yourself you're allowed to name and reframe them as you go through life growing and evolving.

Designing your life can be anything from an attitude to an approach, everything from a way of thinking about your life to handling the details of it. Design is always about being deliberate—remembering this is *your* life, your own beautiful life—to create the life you want intentionally and, yes, with lots of self-permission.

You can say "no" to:

- miring yourself in inaction and regret because you won't own your authority.
- resisting exploration because other options feel too unfamiliar.
- doing what's always been done when you don't want to do it.
- sleepwalking through your days hoping to buy secure years.
- taking the most familiar path when it's not interesting.
- disliking what you're doing but still doing it anyway.

Saying yes to any of these is undesirable, but taken together, they're a recipe for the miserable midlife you want to avoid and can avoid now more than ever. In a fluid world, they're equally a recipe for stagnation and irrelevance, where doing what's always been done likely means you won't have anything to do anymore.

Here are some rules to follow as you imagine your grand design.

Four Rules of Good Life Design

1. **Good design merges what you want with what works.**

Design is intentionally creating something that's both beautiful and functional, something you want, and something that works. It's a marriage of form and function that evolves over time. Design isn't about dreaming of a life in Bali or opening a restaurant when you don't have the resources—time, money, network—to do those things. Less radical, more intentional design is about setting yourself up to flourish, continually balancing desirability and utility to find the beautiful space in the middle.

2. **Life design means ongoing adaptation.**

Design is neither a one-and-done lifetime map you draw for yourself nor thinking that you can have all the pieces in place right away. Instead, design creates the foundations to support your continued evolution, a work in progress, a series of subtle adaptations and upgrades that are fluid, not fixed. Good life design accepts that there will be different versions of you over your lifetime and career and positions you for ongoing development by creating the foundations for a rich and satisfying life, ready to ride the waves of change in a world that promises to never stay the same.

3. **Design means using what works best uniquely.**

Good design merges what works best with what's always worked to produce your unique way; it's not exotic or deliberately "other." Whether you're a stay-at-home parent, an AI prompter, or an architect, if you want it and it works, combine the best of what's always been with what could be, the tried-and-true methods with the try-it-out methods, to create something uniquely you.

4. **Good design is easier than renovation.**

Good design means getting clear about what you want as early or as soon as you can and building your capability to make choices, to be willing to act and redirect, to prepare yourself to change, to adapt, to grow over time.

The challenges of midlife reinvention overwhelm even the most disgruntled adults because even the unhappiest and most discontented souls can get swamped by inertia, the stranglehold of status and responsibility, the debts and assets that need servicing. Whatever agency those adults exercised early in life now feels nostalgic. Whatever they thought they were designing so many years back is now cracked and leaking. Instead of accepting cracks and leaks, you can embed an expectation of change and growth into your life design.

While you can't guarantee yourself a happy ending, your chances for a joyful ride grow exponentially with room to move. I'm not saying things won't wear out or break, but you'll feel capable and resourceful enough to manage your own repairs while understanding that good life design only gets harder with time. So get the fundamentals right as early as you can and, from there, commit to continually adapting.

Pursue Satisfaction Alongside Social Standing

Status is the elephant in this book. If we don't name it and reflect on it, status will make decisions for you, thus making these *Ten Permissions* feel pointless. In the old logic of the fixed world, you engineered your life to achieve status. Every "supposed to" was about gaining status in those systems you were meant to work with all your overachieving might. You'd design your life for someone else's idea of status without even being clear why.

Old logic made status-seeking feel organic, natural even. Who didn't fight for the corner office or crave the McMansion? Not wanting those status symbols was almost a sign of weakness, a lack of ambition, and made you feel like a loser. The desire for status trumped any other desire you might have had but felt too afraid to name or act on. Meaning, connection, and satisfaction all came second to how you were seen, the standing you had in the community, family, or company, which likely led to some poor life choices or ugly life design, like:

- driving up debt to buy stuff.
- sticking with unfulfilling jobs.
- staying in unhappy relationships.
- burning out to scale hierarchal ladders.
- sacrificing ethics for personal advancement.

Ugly life design leads to miserable people locked inside shiny lifestyles, always chasing the next things to feel complete. Maybe you know some of these people. Maybe you need to decide if you still want to be one of them.

New logic: Don't let your desire for status squash your other critical desires.

The quest for standing is as imprinted on us as any other element of our generation's old success stories. Status-chasing can, of course, also lead to all kinds of personal growth and advancement if it's held in balance with your other wants, if you don't get seduced by it, sucked in by the lure of it, and stuck once you've got it. I won't tell you to avoid seeking power and influence or to shun nice things or top positions. Instead, I invite you to get explicit and intentional about your take on status and its role in this fluid world.

Hierarchical, traditional institutions and systems prize and prioritize rank and standing, telling you to chase and secure status as your primary aim because you gain power through your place in the pecking order. It also assumes you want that power and want to hold onto it however you can for as long as you can. But status is an outside game, an extrinsic pursuit, in which you accept other people's metrics of your success. Satisfaction, however, is an inside job, an intrinsic pursuit in which you prize and prioritize what has meaning and value to you.

First, what does status look like to you, and what are you willing to sacrifice to achieve it? Is it what you own? Your salary or your title? Ask yourself, with curiosity and care, what matters to you and why, what you expect status to offer you, and how you expect to feel when you have it. Remember that so much of permission-giving is sitting in conversation with yourself, sitting with what's at stake for you and what you're afraid of, so you're clear on the story you're carrying with you versus the one you're writing—what you want versus what you think you're supposed to want.

A life filled with supposed-to-want-but-don't-want is not a life you want at all. It's full but empty, shiny but dull. It's stuck in a script you didn't write without any ability to write your own. That's not good design. Creating awareness and observing how it plays out over time will serve you as you navigate desire and permission throughout your life.

Second, consider whether status in the fluid world serves you like it did in the fixed world. In the fluid world, status looks different and comes from unlikely places, taking on forms that look unfamiliar to older generations: The young woman without a college degree can catch fire on social media; the guy who owns a chain of lawn care companies can earn more than someone in an air-conditioned office. Status in the fluid world doesn't play by the old rules, so why should you?

More than ever, people are shunning old status games to play their own game, refusing to look for social standing within a system and, instead, seeking satisfaction in their own lives. In the fluid world, having a life you want is the biggest high-status move you can make and may be the only one that matters. So give yourself permission to have the conversation with yourself, to bet on yourself when you decide what's most valued and valuable to you. Then, design a life to deliver that value.

You can. You're allowed.

These *Ten Permissions* will help. Let's get at them.

PART 2

TEN PERMISSIONS FOR A GOOD LIFE

- 1 -

BE WILLFUL

OLD LOGIC: Desire is dangerous
(and will distract you from a safe and secure life).
New logic: Desire is your driver
(and will direct your ever-changing best life).

If 1980s logic wondered where "want" would get you in the fixed world, 21st-century logic says you won't go anywhere in this fluid world without knowing what you want. Taking that one bold step further, knowing what you want and putting yourself behind it can get you almost anywhere in this fluid world because desire transforms the Unraveling into the Renaissance, takes you from desperately searching for security in fickle institutions to locating it in yourself and letting it take you where you want to go.

Desire directs you through your vast sea of life options, showing you what's possible when you pursue who you want to be and what you want to become, what you want to experience, to create, which means knowing what you want and believing that you're allowed to use *your* desires, and not anyone else's, as your guide. Being willful means backing yourself, understanding that burying your desires under everyone else's is neither good life strategy nor the starting point of your success story.

You've got baggage around "will" and "want." I know; I get it: Being a "willful child" wasn't exactly a compliment. Permit yourself to flip that old willful script because good life design starts with desire: Create something *you* want and something that works for *you*.

Your best relationships all started with, or were shaped by, mutual desire. And if wanting something—if desire—makes you uncomfortable, ask yourself why, because desire is a fundamental human driver that calls up our best talents and forges our most meaningful connections.

The best things in your life have been borne of desire, and your best life should be too. And it can be—when you learn to tap into and use your will.

NEW LOGIC IN REAL LIFE

1. See yourself as a free agent.

High agency, free agent—you get where I'm going here.

Maybe you're wondering why I suggest you make a precarious life even more precarious by living life like a free agent. After all, free agency means hustle. It's the athlete looking for a contract, the freelancer patching together enough to pay the rent. Free agency reeks of drifting and insecurity. Right?

Reframing "free agency" for the 21st century looks like being a high-agency human designing your path one desire at a time, intentionally responding to your evolving wants alongside a changing world, and owning your ability and authority to design your life, not by attaching yourself to a single identity or institution for protection, but by trusting your ability to navigate the chaotic marketplace that is this world: Claim your power while you enhance your security.

Your instinct in fluidity is to look for something fixed: the most ironclad contract, the industry that looks AI proof. You want to build a bigger life raft because you think that's how you'll ride out the waves of change and uncertainty. Why not learn to swim instead? Better yet, float. Dive in when it's deep enough.

You may have thought you had to give up power to gain security, but you don't, not in the Renaissance, where the radical offer is to combine autonomy, satisfaction, and security in the same career. This is only possible if you embrace your own free agency.

Don't fight fluidity; learn to flow with it. Figure out how to work with it to discover more options and possibilities than you had before, more than you thought were allowed. Meet fluidity with more fluid life strategies via free agency.

Free agency recognizes that the world of work is ever more fluid and disconnected from fixedness than it has been in the past. Living a 9-to-5, five-days-a-week job, is increasingly rare. Layoffs are on the rise; roles are being replaced by artificial intelligence. Clutching for fixedness is futile, the sense of security illusory. You're better off detaching your sense of security from any single company, contract, role, or position and attaching it to *yourself.*

You are your own agent, authorized to design your own way forward through a fluid world and disrupted work patterns. You're driven and you're driving, choosing the nature and direction of your path, and able to negotiate around a clear and ever-evolving set of wants. When you make your own choices routinely as the world evolves, you routinely choose situations that work for *you*, as well as for the new rules of society.

The idea that you'll intentionally evolve yourself over the course of your life or that you'll be driven by what you want in the process may feel radical, scary, abnormal. If you're feeling uncomfortable, have a good look at what's prickling you. Remember the old logic doesn't work anymore, and you don't want it anyway because it's not good design.

Repeat after me: Security is not holding onto the status quo for as long as I can. Security is confidence in my ability to evolve with the world. The world will change. I will change. I will *want to* change. And that desire for and need to change is not a threat, but an opportunity.

These are not radical statements; they're patently obvious. Permit yourself to work with current reality intentionally and boldly by taking the free-agency proposition, by seeing it as an attitude as much as a strategy. Free agency is rooted in the realities of a fluid world, where stability is found in flexibility and your ability to adapt to rapid, high-volume change, which means freeing up your identity from the two things that used to give it shape: conformity and uniformity.

Free agents know they've got to shine. Old logic wanted you to fit into fixed hierarchies and the uniformity of ready-made roles, but free agency means knowing why you're unique. Uniquely valuable, capable, able. Own it. Feel it. Allow yourself to believe that the most unique version of you is the one that's allowed to show up and, most likely, to succeed. You don't have to self-limit to succeed; you can allow yourself to stand out, to shine, and to find the places that want exactly what you can offer.

Instead of seeing yourself as a "worker" who fills a company role, you're an agent selling your capabilities to different institutions and people over time.

Sometimes, free agency will look exactly like a 9-to-5 job, but it'll be a job you're ready to evolve out of when necessary, taking your portfolio of clients, capabilities, or roles with you. As a willful free agent, you intentionally gather experiences and resources to make you ever more capable of riding out disruption and change. You're creating your own resource portfolio.

Once you accept that having one long-term or lifetime source of employment and income won't guarantee security, start curating a portfolio of resources that you'll deploy throughout your life and career to help you manage change, like:

- **networks**—people and contacts
- **assets**—money, goods, investments
- **skills**—technical, field-specific knowledge
- **experiences**—exposure to a range of contexts and situations
- **capabilities**—not technical skills but abilities that serve you in and out of work

Traditionally, historically, you might have only been intentional about your assets, but that's not enough anymore. You must be deliberate about what you're learning, where you're working, whom you're meeting, and what you're doing, with an eye not only on what's being offered today but also how those offers prepare you for tomorrow, how future fit and flexible you'll be to adapt and change when you need and want to. Your portfolio is your leverage: What do I know? Who do I know? How much of a risk can I afford to take? By building a robust, diverse portfolio, you'll stave off anxiety and insecurity, trading them in for robust, nimble, and patient responsiveness and resourcefulness.

This kind of *portfolio approach* to life and career is alive and well and all around you. According to the freelancing marketplace Upwork, half the US workforce will be freelancing by 2027. More and more people don't want to "put all their eggs in one basket" and are choosing freelancing and consulting for two main reasons:

- People no longer view long-term full-time employment with a company as secure.
- People are looking for more satisfying, fulfilling careers over time.[1]

Building out your portfolio means willfully and intentionally combining different roles, gigs, and employers to secure both growth and security, to continually pursue the audacious proposition that you can, that you're allowed, and that you're in control. You're designing your career, driving its trajectory. You're allowed to accept that full-time permanence is no longer the ideal in highly disruptive environments where people value autonomy and flexibility and companies value access to talent that fills specific needs. Where

1 "Freelancing Meets Gen Z Modern Work Needs," Upwork, May 14, 2024, https://www.upwork.com/research/gen-z-work-requirements.

multiple clients and income streams might not only limit your risk exposure but also accelerate your growth and ongoing success.

You don't want to get stuck with narrow experiences, limited exposure, a small network, and an aversion to the new. Your parents or grandparents might not have worried about being stuck, but you do; you should. The portfolio approach builds unstuckedness into your life design by providing you a clear-eyed commitment to hone your value and relevance and becoming more flexible so you can meet specific and changing needs. While living in a volatile world where you'll face change, engineer your life (or your company) for greater responsiveness to and flexibility in whatever way works best. Seek out opportunities, which will look different for everyone and different over time, to make your best contributions.

The key to free agency is willfully designing a life that meets your (and the world's) evolving desires.

You must keep asking yourself:

- What kind of situation do I want to work in?
- What do I want to learn or how do I want to grow?
- Do I want to change my situation to accommodate my (or the world's) changes?

Ask yourself these questions and *answer* them rather than pondering and then ignoring them because you're worried you might blow up your life. That's inertia when you're after free agency.

Free agency involves:

- driving your career evolution.

- being clear about how you add value.
- negotiating with clear desire and intent.
- resourcefully managing change and disruption.
- recognizing and responding to your changing needs.
- actively building your capabilities, skills, and networks.
- scanning your environment for threats and opportunities.
- walking away from what you don't want and walking toward what you do.

Moving with and through situations that you want and that work in this world while avoiding becoming stuck in situations you don't want and that don't work. Sounds audacious? Greedy? No. Strategic.

2. Look for the right fit rather than trying to fit in.

Seeking to meet mutual needs and creating shared value, the free agent is on the lookout for the right fit, not trying to fit in. While the old logic had you figuring out what a company wanted and shaping yourself to fit the need, the new logic says you must figure out your value-add and find situations where you are needed. Lean into your unique portfolio of skills, capabilities, and experiences to find the person who needs it.

Is this outlook transactional? Maybe. But it's also ripe with potential for growth and satisfaction because finding the right fit makes for more desirable, mutually satisfying situations and outcomes. You're permitting yourself to make your best contributions by acting from your clearest sense of desire and showing up as the most valued and valuable form of yourself.

You become a better negotiator, a more generous partner, a more imaginative creator when you're not sacrificing some part of yourself by trying to fit in. You accelerate your growth and learning by moving to and through situations that will present new opportunities and challenges each time. You don't outsource approval to every new situation you're in, and you don't make everyone you meet the arbiter of your value.

And you don't stick around too long. Giving yourself permission to move on when the fit is no longer good is critical.

Your wants, like anyone else's, change over time. You grow out of things, and there's no shame in that. Your changing wants aren't an inconvenience or a threat to your security; they're fuel for your success. They're an opportunity to grow. Holding onto situations long after you've outgrown them is how you get stuck; it's where misery is born.

Finding the right fit means:

- cultivating your communication and negotiation capabilities.
- keeping a life network of opportunities and contacts.
- candidly assessing fit and value over time.
- having and respecting clear boundaries.
- knowing what your offer is.
- creating shared value.

Being a cog in a machine is old logic. You're not just generating resources. You *are* a resource. Sounds radical, right? But your lot in life isn't just to work at a desk for someone else's profit. You may sit at a desk and make a company profit, of course, but you're there willfully making something else as well: money, learning, connections, growth. Your life isn't a machine, you're not a cog, and your options are limitless.

3. See yourself as potent, not problematic.

Present to the world your best offers and most valuable contributions. Are your alarm bells going off? Does this whole free-agent/find-the-right-fit thing sound self-serving and entitled? Is your inner critic shouting, "Who do you think you are, going out there and designing a life based on your changing wants? Who do you think you are, refusing to get a good job, put your head down, and save up for material possessions? Who *do* you think you are?"

Is that how all of this sounds to you?

Free agency sounds like all the desire and none of the dutiful adult compliance, and that's likely to ring all the good-boy-and-girl alarm bells, to spark the fears of being greedy and self-interested and absorbed, which makes sense given that you've probably been brought up with an old-logic playbook.

Free agency looks nothing like your parents' or grandparents' lives or career strategies. Most of them never dreamed of doing this kind of stuff. Having a life driven by desire wasn't what successful people did. That kind of lifestyle was either for strays and losers or, on the flip side, special people: elites, artists, and athletes. You were meant to slip into a role and do the same thing for the rest of your life to buy you the lifetime certainty, predictability, and security you were meant to crave.

We've allowed ourselves to believe that we should be satisfied being able to pay our bills and scraping by, but that's old logic and has no place in the fluid world. You're allowed meaning and satisfaction and expression and excellence, which don't have to be obtained on the biggest stages of the world by only the biggest stars in the world. They're yours as well. But they only come through when you connect to your desires and find your fit in the world.

Will you always get what you want? No.

Will you be able to articulate everything you want? No.

Will acting on your wants mean you always get a happy ending? No.

But understanding and acting on your desire means you're showing up as the best version of yourself, ready to make your best contribution, and find the people you want to do it for and with. Then, listening to their wants while expressing your own, you learn and get feedback about how you can grow along with a world that's changing so rapidly you're required to do the same.

YOU ALREADY KNOW THIS.

In case this talk of willful desire has you rattled, remember what you already know about desire and its role in the world.

In sports, for instance, the phrase "How much do you want it?" is almost cliché. Inner drive and desire are critical to achieving goals, if not greatness. Go back to your own life, to the things you want and love and like the most: your favorite class, your best friend, and a place you kept wanting to go back to. You felt something when you showed up. You were alive when you were there, in those moments. That's what desire is—the lifeblood of vitality.

Once you stop feeling desire, you stop feeling alive. And then you're stuck. Don't get stuck. Instead, harness your desires. Feel them! Permit yourself to act on them, not as a whim but as a strategy.

AVOID THIS: REGRET.

Moreover, avoid the regret of unfulfilled want and inaction, the regret of what you wanted to say, do, experience, or create but were too afraid because of what might happen, what others might think, and the fear of failing. You wanted to go for it but didn't. You wanted to try it but didn't. You wanted to make it but didn't. You wanted to get out but wouldn't leave. Regret sacrifices "want" to "what if," bottling up desire due to fear of what might happen.

Anybody over age forty will tell you regret sucks. It can't be corrected. There are no rewinds or redos. And because regret is all the things you *didn't* do, not all the things you did, repression fuels regret far more than risk does. Not doing what you want never made anybody happy or satisfied, and it's not a strategy for success either. It's a strategy for stuck. Don't do stuck.

- 2 -

GO ASTRAY

Old logic: Protect the status quo at all costs.

New logic: Adapt or die.

If the straightest path used to be the safest one, now it's probably the least secure or strategic. It's likely going nowhere except toward regret and irrelevance. If engineering your life for flexibility, then a linear life path—minimize change, avoid risk, stay in your lane—doesn't cut it. A linear life path is rigid when you want bendy, narrow when you're allowed to spread out. It's sameness when you want diversity, a flat line rather than a beating heart.

In a fast-changing world requiring peak adaptability, it's time to accept that "linear" is not the good life path you've been sold. More than that, linearity might be the most anti-adaptable life choice you can make because it casts your sense of identity and capability in stone and prioritizes protecting the status quo when you need to get used to dealing with the different.

In a world demanding flexibility, linearity sees you getting narrow and stiff, limiting your exposure to new experiences, interests, and skills. When you need to be more resourceful and robust, the linear life story leaves you vulnerable: Your curiosity and imagination get stunted by sameness; your appetite for risk is starved. Your peripheral vision switches off because you're only looking right in front of you. You get complacent. You stop learning.

You get stuck.

Loops are unstuck, loose and fluid, embracing change rather than tolerating it. Loops embed permission into designing what your life looks like, what routine evolution looks like.

NEW LOGIC IN REAL LIFE

1. Design a loopy life.

Don't wait to be thrown off course, resisting change until you can't hold on any longer. Intentionally design loops into your life to maximize learning and growth.

Don't see your life as a straight line or even a straight line with a few shifts.

See it (want it and design it) as a loopy, curvy line, the sign of your 21st-century good life.

I know. I know. You're supposed to imagine a good life as some neat, sequential adult ascendance toward ever greater money and power, a cool one-thing-leads-to-the-next shout-out to loyalty and discipline, compliance, and virtue. Who pictures a loopy up-and-down life? Drunks wobble. Strays set out. Losers go looking. Who would consciously create a loopy life?

You would. You will!

Engineer your good life to prepare for a lifetime of disruptive change by choosing a life with loops. Loops look like your life taking a turn, a whole new direction, a pause, a meander, a retracing of steps, or a quest. Anything other than the straight and narrow, the gradual and sequential.

Loops represent you finding your way through new life territory, evolving through phases and opportunities, growing in and out of things, all the while consciously building your capacity to continually adapt to a rapidly changing environment. You can't see where your path heads much less ends, especially when you're steering through the obstacles in front of you. Intentionally embedding change in your life helps you future-proof yourself in a world in which the path of your future is obscured. You're building your change management muscle, preparing yourself for changes you know will come but can't yet see.

Repeat after me: Preparedness trumps predictability.

In an unpredictable world, the best you can do is nurture your own preparedness, setting aside—but not shunning—concerns that you don't know what your future looks like. Sure, you're making your life look more like the unpredictable world, but you're also making the world look more like the life you want. Maybe not knowing what your future looks like is not such a bad thing—*if* you prepare yourself.

What you see as detours from a straight life path are, in fact, learning accelerators. Every time you stop something old or start something new, you learn. Every time you pause for a birth or a death, you learn. Every time you intentionally turn left or right, you learn because you confront something new.

If you need time to make a move—to accelerate yourself in a new direction instead of being frog-marched forward—you may. Whenever you're worried that a change will stall or stop your progress on the neat line of your life, consider whether it's time for a learning loop. Allow yourself to change direction and trust your new direction will teach you something.

One key thing you'll learn? How to deal with discomfort.

You've probably been told to "get out of your comfort zone" a lot, which, though it may sound like sky diving or rock climbing, means dealing with the discomfort of starting something new, confronting something different, or leaving the familiar behind.

Discomfort is:

- not knowing what you're doing.
- being the newcomer or the beginner.
- finding your way through new spaces.
- meeting new people or making new friends.

You don't know whether you can do something, whether you'll like something, or what it will feel like, but all of that not knowing, *all of it*, is critical for you to navigate a disruptive world. You must learn how to hold those feelings, face them, and treat them not as a reason to turn back or stay put but to keep going.

Maybe you think you don't want to learn how to deal with discomfort, that discomfort isn't what you're signing up for. But if you want to feel alive, to learn, to grow, to love, and to experience the best that life has to offer, you must become comfortable with discomfort.

Because that's how you go about:

Building adaptability: When you head in a new direction, you confront the new; you choose it! You want it, you go after it, you're not afraid of it, you welcome it. (Permission Four's got a lot to say about not being afraid. We'll get there soon.) Every loop you design in your life lessens your fear of the new and different, making you more robust and ready for whatever comes your way. You don't cling to a straight line; you're ready to ride the waves of change because you've been riding them your whole life. You're changing by design, not by default, because you want to.

Keeping your options open: You're only as prepared and secure as the options you have available. So your job, your focus, is to continually nurture your options, not to see your current one as the only one or the only best one. You're a free agent who's available, alive to opportunities, and looking for good fits, so you must make yourself available to new options by scanning your environment, remaining open to new ideas and ways of doing things, meeting new players in your field, and keeping up to date on what's happening. You must be adaptable.

Adaptability means you're confident and decisive enough to:

- **stop something:** I know you've got to feed yourself and pay your bills, but you're also allowed to quit, to leave, to say, "No, no more." You can let go of a good thing because you trust the possibility of a great thing.
- **start something:** You can also say, "Yes!" to the untested and untried, the I'm-not-sure-how-this-is-going-to-go-but-I'm-moving-forward-anyway real-time testing of the new.

- **start over:** You may go back to the beginning and see the return as progress. Your sense of moving forward is far more nuanced than a straight arrow.
- **go deeper:** Dig in, learn, invest your resources, and stake a claim in something you want to build on or grow with.
- **shoot higher:** Go for it; go after it, whatever it is. It's not reckless to want more for your life and world unless you don't have the resources to ride the waves of change.
- **rest:** Just rest. It's OK. You're allowed.

Will you always make the right choices? No, of course not, but you will make choices you want and choices you trust without hesitating or overthinking as you wrestle with desires you fear you're not allowed to have. You're active, decisive, and aligned, and when you act from that place, the "correctness" of your decisions is less important than your willingness to make them, while acknowledging that your learning loops will look different as you progress through life. A veritable tangle in your twenties as you work through what you want and how to get it, which softens as you age into confidence that you're choosing the right loops.

When you go astray and design your loopy life, you avoid flatlining, at least, avoid it for long periods of time. Flat lines not only often indicate lack of growth and learning, but they can also be a sign of sleepwalking if you're not careful. Remember, the loopy life is like a heartbeat, and sometimes it will be spiky, ragged, with big ups and downs. It'll feel messy, and you'll feel all kinds of bad boy or girl for the mess. But the mess is OK if it brings discomfort and not danger. Just like a spiked heart rate, that means you're experiencing something. You're under pressure. You must work, which might not be comfortable, but it means you're alive. Feeling alive is the antidote to being stuck.

2. Think in terms of "I can" rather than "I am."

One of the reasons you get stuck in that straight-line life mentality is because you're told to pick a profession out of school and stick with it, presumably for the rest of your life. Old logic cast you in an "I am" identity—I am a doctor, teacher, plumber, dancer—and expected you to spend the rest of your life with that definition. As a free agent, though, you switch your mindset from "I am" to "I can," so you may see yourself not as a single external identity or role but as an ever-evolving set of capabilities that can be applied in different contexts over time.

Why?

In the fluid and disrupted world of work, what were once full-time jobs are now being pulled apart into smaller tasks or projects—work to be done rather than roles to be filled. Companies are trimming fat. Increasingly, artificial intelligence focuses on outcomes, competitive advantages, and who can do what, and it will continue to challenge our understandings of ourselves as fixed roles or full-time positions, eating away at labels like doctor, lawyer, or accountant as full-time proprietary identities that have built-in security. In this challenging marketplace, you must unbundle your identity from any single "I am" profession to become a complex and evolving set of capabilities. You must become adaptive, open to new opportunities and applications, and nimble enough to prize skills over positions and periodic opportunities over full-time roles, which can sound either terrifying or ripe with possibilities. It could feel like the unraveling of your safety net or the Renaissance of your best self.

"I can" recognizes that you will, of course, still play in traditional professional roles without being defined by them because your attention focuses on the skills and capabilities that allow you to fill those roles. And you'll see the work of your life not as holding onto a single title or role, but routinely augmenting and evolving your set of capabilities.

"I can" finds security in capabilities and status in responding to what you don't know rather than wielding what you do. It recognizes that the only way to thrive in this joyride of a world is by turning "I am" into "I can."

With an "I can" mindset, you're more confident finding your way than following the leader. Your head is up and looking for the next option on the road or in the distance, trusting capability and anticipation over certainty and predilection so you don't feel you need to know what comes next to be ready to face it. It's preparedness over prediction.

Intentionally building your "I can" mentality means (drumroll, please) building a portfolio of skills and capabilities, a collection of assets that help you feel ready. No matter your life path or chosen profession, you're consciously and intentionally building your portfolio to help you ride out disruption and leverage possibility. (Even doctors these days have side hustles and aren't safe from disruption.) Because anything is possible in this Renaissance. Robustness lives in "I can" and gives you the confidence as a free agent to venture off the straight path in the service of building a diverse portfolio of experiences and capabilities, a readiness for change, a preparedness for the unpredictable.

Three types of skills to add to your fluid-world portfolio are:

1. **Portable skills** applicable across industries, jobs, or sectors, both evergreen and of-this-moment skills: Writing, improvisation, and negotiation are always needed. Add in graphic design and video editing, and you're even more valuable. Be conscious of building and having useful skills and amplify your willingness and ability to apply them across industries.
2. **Unique skills**, or skills that are uniquely you and reach into your deep knowledge, your do-it-all-the-time knowledge, your do-it-better-than-anybody knowledge. It's your firmest of footings *and* your flow state. Nurture deep knowledge throughout your life even when you feel like you can do whatever it is you do best in your sleep. Keep updating what you know and have and get curious about what you can do with that knowledge and skill in different contexts.
3. **Passion skills** you love and live for, even those that aren't expressly job related. One day, that passion skill may be relevant for you. Maybe you'll make it a Thing with a capital *T*. Maybe it will introduce you to someone, or maybe it'll keep reintroducing you to yourself. Nurture what you're passionate about to keep reminding yourself where pleasure sits for you, how desire lives in your life. Passion must be a part of you that shows up to all the beautiful places you'll visit as you go astray. And the skills you develop in following your passion will always be translatable to other areas of your life.

As you build your resource portfolio, desire drives: What do I want to learn? How do I want to grow? What opportunities do I want to create for myself? How do I want to take advantage of change and disruption? When desire drives, you create adaptable expertise to apply in emerging or evolving contexts. Instead of a fixed "this is what I know" mindset, you're approaching life with "here's how I'm able to apply my knowledge" nimbly and resourcefully as you look for those emerging options.

3. Always be on the lookout for your next best option.

Building your diverse portfolio of knowledge and skills means that, as you move through your life and career, you deliberately seek out what is different rather than what is familiar, but "different" may be incremental, not far out on the horizon or far from your comfort zone. Going too far may not be in your best interest. It's OK to think in terms of adjacent rather than afar, because each encounter with newness brings new sets of abilities that serve you in unpredictability, a combination of applying what you know in different contexts and consciously trying to know more by learning new skills and seeking out new experiences.

Seek out change so when change comes to you, you're ready. If you continually build, continually broaden your horizons—even incrementally—your lifeline won't stay straight and fixed. It will move in different directions and take you to new places, which is what you want, because the more exposed you are, the more capable you feel.

Remember that your diverse portfolio of capabilities and experiences is the base that gives you the strength to navigate volatility and disruption, helping you realize you're more resourceful than you'd previously imagined.

YOU ALREADY KNOW THIS.

Doing one thing for the rest of your life isn't viable or desirable, but you may not have been able to imagine another way. You don't want the straitjacket of an identity that you're supposed to choose early in life and wear forever, and you don't have to get stuck in it. You can do different things. You can have phases and seasons. You can get bored and restless and curious and hungry, and those are not inconveniences or threats to your stability. They're marks of growth and change and humanity. The beautifully chaotic fluid world can accommodate all those changes and allows you to explore all the facets of who you are and who you're becoming.

Because fear is often the only thing keeping you in that line, that straitjacket of life that says staying in your lane is how you build the best kind of life. But staying in your lane is incompatible with a loopy life.

You don't have to have a singular identity. You can build something better.

You can *be* something better.

AVOID THIS: DRIFTING.

Going astray without knowing why is going adrift—all the loops and none of the desire. It's lack of direction and lack of intention. Don't change for the sake of change; don't look around for the new thing or the next thing without a clear sense of why or how you're looking. You want to learn or grow, but if you find yourself looping without love, go back to your straight line and recalibrate. Stillness may be your friend in that case. Going astray without love or purpose is a strategy for stuck. Don't do stuck.

- 3 -

TAKE IT OUTSIDE

Old logic: Successful adulting is an inside job.

New logic: Thriving adults need to take their lives outside.

Inside is inherently a thinking state, a static state, and often an alone state disconnected from the world. Being an adult has always been an inside job. Your habitat is a world of houses and spouses, offices and desks. Of heads and of beds. The habitat gets progressively smaller as you grow older, more routinized and familiar, because comfort and predictability are what you're meant to crave, because the unfamiliar becomes more irrelevant or dangerous as your life gets more fixed in place.

As we double down on the fixed to shelter from the fluid, we retreat to the safety of home and to the desire for comfort. We order in rather than going out. We keep busy schedules and follow strict disciplines to give us the structure and control lacking "out there." We experience the world through the interface of our phones as real life gets more overwhelming and foreboding, the outside not only a distraction but a threat.

It's wild out there!

Your instinct is to turn inward for safety, to find comfort and a sense of power in the variables you can control. But it's not working. Insularity and isolation are not making you feel stronger based on current rates of burnout[1] and anxiety.[2] Not if you look at skyrocketing obesity,[3] at rampant loneliness and rising suicide rates.[4]

Inside, we're prone to languishing and rumination. We move too little and think too much.

Our 21st-century inside lives look like:

- immersion in information but isolation from human connection.
- highly opinionated but hugely inexperienced people.
- small analog lives within a digital sprawl.
- knowing much but living little.

Your inside-oriented adult is brittle in the face of the unfamiliar and uncomfortable because the internal habitat is engineered

---

1 Preeti Vankar, "Percentage of Employees in the United States by Current Level of Burnout as of 2023," *Statista*, December 19, 2023, https://www.statista.com/statistics/1383756/current-level-of-burnout-us-employees/.

2 "Any Anxiety Disorder," *National Institute of Mental Health*, accessed December 2024, https://www.nimh.nih.gov./health/statistics/any-anxiety-disorder.

3 "Adult Obesity Facts," Obesity, *CDC*, May 14, 2024, https://www.cdc.gov/obesity/adult-obesity-facts/index.html.

4 Gonzalo Martinez-Ales, Daniel Hernandez-Calle, Nicole Khauli, and Katherine M. Keyes, "Why Are Suicide Rates Increasing in the United States? Towards a Multilevel Reimagination of Suicide Prevention." *Current Topics in Behavioral Neurosciences* 46 (2020): 1–23. DOI: 10.1007/7854_2020_158.

for ease. It's climate-controlled. Once you step out of that neat, circumscribed space, you may not know how to cope with the new, the other, the unfamiliar. All the inside-ness breeds anti-adaptability and makes the wild feel even wilder. If we let our inside-oriented adults rule, we feel less capable of dealing with the fluid world outside.

If thriving in the 21st century means engineering for fluidity, then sheltering in place doesn't make sense. Fluid is motion, boundlessness; it's coming and going, up and down. Sitting still won't work because stillness can't immunize against fluidity.

We're hiding from the world we need to step into, the world we need to encounter and explore not to feel better—not as a pastime (though there's nothing wrong with doing things that bring enjoyment and relaxation) but to thrive. If we want to learn, to grow, to adapt, to translate the Unraveling into Renaissance, then we have to take our lives outside.

Outside is a metaphor for both everything beyond the known—the familiar, routine, and everyday—and the world outside the door—your home, office, and head.

Permission to take it outside is permission to believe that your life doesn't have to be small to be safe. You don't have to live in isolation. Maybe you don't even have to be so scared because you can allow some desired wildness back into your life.

Grant self-permission to design a life that doesn't have big walls or fences, whether real or imagined, and whether they protect your property or your identity—a life that's expansive, active, and intentional.

NEW LOGIC IN REAL LIFE

1. Think more like an explorer, less like an executive.

Channel your inner willful explorer, that high-agency human willing to step out in the world and put one foot in front of the other—the one who sees possibility where others see threat, the one who quests while others stay put. While the executive rode high in the fixed world, the explorer is the archetype of the fluid world because the explorer's habitat is naturally outside spaces that feel marked and known.

Your inner explorer knows that success isn't about executing on the known but stepping into the unknown. It's not about building fragile walls of certainty but cultivating your ability to flourish amidst uncertainty. You're willing to step into what you don't know while remaining curious and pragmatic, resourceful and persistent. You've got discomfort tolerance for days. OK, maybe minutes, but even a few minutes is better than not having tolerance for discomfort at all. To go looking is one of the hallmarks of high agency: to avoid waiting for things to be presented to you, to avoid accepting only what's right in front of you.

Optimism is inherent in the willingness to go looking, a belief in better, an interest in deeper, and a receptiveness to the other. You want an answer, an option, an inspiration, an alternative. You want something you don't currently have or know, and so you go looking. Desire drives the quest.

Exploring isn't straight lines to known destinations; it's finding your way to and through the known and familiar and toward the unknown and desirable. As you start looking, you go astray: What are you looking for? What's possible? What's the next best option? What's just beyond your line of vision?

One of the most pernicious qualities of the inside life is that it stunts your ability to solve problems because you face so few. Things break and lightbulbs need to be changed, of course, but for the most part, life is fairly friction free. The slightest difficulty or obstacle can then quickly feel overwhelming. You replace things rather than fixing them, outsourcing your hassles. You weaken your ability to critically engage with things that don't work, things that you haven't seen before, that don't come with instructions or directions. By cutting yourself off from the things that threaten you, you also cut yourself off from what teaches, nourishes, and makes you feel alive.

Being able to figure things out is critical in a fluid world, just as critical thinking is a superpower in an artificial intelligence world. You must face novel problems, deal with uncomfortable challenges, and test your capabilities, which hardly happens inside.

The outside is predictably unpredictable and full of potential with new:

- experiences to have.
- problems to solve.
- people to meet.
- skills to learn.
- joy to feel.

Forget your fear of the new and unfamiliar. Better, seek out fear, step into it, because you know it's where potential lies. Step outside where newness lives. Even similar experiences will be tinged with new variables.

Your inner willful explorer is inherently and intuitively active, figuring out the next step and finding a way. The explorer steps outside and away from scrolling, navel-gazing, how-abouting, and what-iffing. The explorer is curious about action and reaction, push and pull: When you yell at someone, they yell back at you; when you tell somehow how you feel, you witness their response. Put yourself in an *active learning state*, a continual process of stepping into the new even when your steps are tiny.

Prize action over rumination because action accelerates learning by producing new information, feedback, and insights. The minute you step outside of your familiar spaces, you make a whole bunch of tiny choices as you drive your path and decide your course of action. Whether that's down a new street or up a mountain, putting yourself into new outside spaces determines the direction of your forward motion by stretching your reference points and creating openings for more, different, and next.

Each new step forward is a new experience, a fresh perspective, a different angle. Big and small strides, even seemingly insignificant decisions, stretch out your range of motion, expanding your understanding of yourself and your world—what you know, what you think we're capable of, and how far you think we're allowed to roam.

By expanding your reference points and making your life bigger, you extend your options, and your portfolio of experiences grows wider so you can make new choices and spot new things, while avoiding being starved of options and ideas, like a body starved of energy.

Action is the antidote to fear. Fear lives in your imagination, in what-if and in how-about. Anxiety breeds in inaction. And the only thing to counter that is concrete action that produces a reaction, real-time feedback. As you drive ahead and act, you become less afraid and start separating discomfort from danger, figuring out what's imagined and what's real. Taking a walk by yourself or taking a train to an unvisited part of the city probably isn't as scary as you thought. The only way to find out is to try.

Going outside doesn't need to involve oversized amounts of courage or daring: more toddler, less mountain climber. You don't have to go to the woods. You just have to go beyond the spaces you normally roam in. One step will do. And then another. You did it when you were a kid. You had to learn how to walk and run and color and create. You were a little explorer at one time. You can be again. You must!—if you're going to get comfortable again with the new and never-done-before so that you learn, expand your life rather than contract it, and tap into your willingness to step beyond the known and familiar and believe in "out there" again and its inherent promise.

2. Get a hobby!

Historically, we've designed leisure and hobbies out of our adult lives. At the very least, we defaulted to the idea that work was our primary responsibility and the primary expression of our value. The old logic told you to get a job, but it deprioritized getting a hobby. Executives didn't have hobbies. Who had time for unserious business when they were head-down inside implementing plans and having meetings and making money? But your job doesn't have to be your primary expression of value.

We've been told that we are our work, that our work must be us. And so we lose ourselves in it and, in the process, we lose the vastness of our lives to it. Yet leisure is a critical conduit for agency and desire, and when you switch it off, you switch off so many potential desires and capabilities.

This vast and fluid world offers so many ways for us to learn and grow and connect and create, which is not to say you shouldn't find work you love or enjoy. Rather, work isn't the *only* way you find joy and meaning and satisfaction and connection in the world.

People tend to think their job has to be an extension of them, a replication of them. It can be, but it doesn't have to be. The job can be part of the portfolio, but not the whole thing. Build high-quality leisure time into your life design to take off some pressure and brighten your sense of agency rather than limiting your options and your sense of where and how you learn and grow.

Leisure is agency and desire in action: What do I want to do? To know? To play around with? Leisure is a way to discover your desires and dial up your agency. Leisure is a permissions playground, in which you let yourself find things you really want to do and *do* them, guilt free, because you know leisure activities feed you, stimulate you, and help you show up as your most valuable self regardless of your chosen hobby, as long as you gain a sense of purpose and joy to generate meaning and satisfaction.

Whether purpose and joy come from the thing you get paid for or the thing that you do in your spare time, give yourself permission to believe that your human wholeness is critically important. Leisure takes us outside of our day to day, connects us to others, and reminds us of what we can create.

3. Seek out beauty.

Is that a weird one? What does beauty have to do with thriving in the 21st century?

Everything.

What motivates the inner willful explorer? The search for better, the search for beauty in whatever form that takes, the promise of the boundless world. As consumers, we're always on the lookout for beauty, and we pay top dollar to own it and to show it. Beauty is experience, stimulus, hope.

The inside life cuts you off from the wonder of the world, from an innate and intuitive sense of possibility. The news is all bad. All the worst of being human is displayed: Scandal, shock, horror, and fear come swooping into your inside life via your screen. There's not a lot of space for beauty.

"Wow!" matters. "Look at that!" matters. Awe matters because beauty makes you feel something. Seek out beauty to stimulate and inspire, energize and inform. Beauty reminds you that whatever has you spinning out today hasn't been there as long as trees, the sunrise, mountains, or waves. There are constants. There are reasons for hope and belief.

It's hard to feel much awe when stuck inside a dullness that can make you believe the only way to *feel* something is to *pay* for it—that the most beautiful thing is the one with the latest features, not the thing that's been the same since forever. But the inside life is isolating even if you're not isolated. Be part of something beautiful, part of something bigger, something grand.

Beauty is hope, and it is unafraid.

YOU ALREADY KNOW THIS.

You don't need to be sold on the benefits of leaving your desk, letting life in, or being a part of something bigger. Early in life, you went outside, even if it was just to build forts or make up dance routines in the garage. You did stuff and made stuff with others and on your own. You know how much fun it is to be outside. So many of your best memories are there. But when analyzing success, outside became superfluous. You went out there less and less until the outside became scarier, and you stopped going out.

Remember what it's like to play outside: Stakes are low and joy is high, especially the particular connective joy that comes with playing outside: the laughter, the shrieks, the hugs, and the fist pumps. There's nothing quite like playing outside.

AVOID THIS: BUNKERING.

When you return home, don't hide; rest and reconnect to family, to self, to your interests. Of course, you need comfort. You want it, so savor it, and let it recharge you. But don't let your inside time cut you off from the world. Let it not be a place where you disappear. Make it, instead, a nest that restores you for the next venture out so you don't get stuck. Don't do stuck.

- 4 -

EXPERIMENT

Old logic: If x, then y.

New logic: What if?

Experiment? Sounds a little dodgy, right? What might be great in a lab may not be so great in real life, and certainly not in a responsible adult life in which you're supposed to deal in known quantities and predictable outcomes, in which you must see an upside—and it better be financial.

Experiments sound frivolous or freaky to that responsible-adult brain that shouts, "But what if it goes wrong? What if it doesn't work out?" That responsible-adult brain isn't comfortable when you have no idea how things are going to turn out. What-if questions paralyze that brain with fear; uncertainty shows a reel of all the possible bad outcomes, and you keep hitting replay.

Cue: inertia.

Cue: rumination.

Cue: anxiety and overwhelm.

Flip the script on "what if," and see it as an invitation rather than a warning, a door cracked open with no baddie behind it, a gateway to possibility. You get to reset your relationship to "what if" because in the fluid world, "what if" is a menace of indecision. So work with it. Leverage it. Allow it to inform your Renaissance rather than letting it be your Unraveling by giving yourself permission to experiment and act without certainty, to reframe what "being in control" looks and feels like, to loosen your attachment to predictability. Take "what if" outside and see what's possible when possibilities exist in the external world, not in your head.

Nurturing a more experimental mindset lives in the heart of a thriving 21st-century adult: You take yourself off the straight and narrow path, pursue your desires, find your next best option. You shift from defaulting to designing, from doing what others tell you to doing what you want. From inaction to action. You write your own story, one nurturing experiment and experience at a time.

Experiments are how you explore and prepare for the new. Introduce your good boy or girl to your inner explorer, the same explorer who didn't learn to walk by watching a video, who didn't learn piano by reading a theory book, who fell off your skateboard a hundred times while perfecting a new trick, whose arms flailed as you learned to swim—and it didn't faze you because you felt yourself growing ever more powerful.

Yes, powerful!

Power sits in your willingness to experiment; success sits in the depth of your desire to do so.

NEW LOGIC IN REAL LIFE

1. See your success as a series of experiments.

You want to believe that the best way to navigate adulthood is through a series of rational choices. You want to believe if you just make one or two great choices, then you're set, you're made, you're on a path to financial success. Of course, you want to believe this.

We all want to believe that a few ironclad choices will provide us the certainty and clarity we need to carve our path to success and security. Except that old logic doesn't work anymore. The world doesn't work that way anymore.

Expecting to make your best choices based on available information means you'll encounter big problems because:

- you have too much information and too little clarity.
- you don't have the information you need when you need it.
- you can't rely on existing information but don't know what to trust.
- you don't have a long line of sight and can't see far enough into the future.

You don't live in an if-x-then-y world. The old equations don't always add up, and you can't envision a simple equation for success, which is terrifying because the alternative historically was fraught with danger and loaded with risk, and good adults avoided danger and risk. Two basic cornerstones of the old logic for fixed-world success no longer apply:

I know *where I'll be in five or ten years; that if I study this topic and get this job, then I'm made!* But you're not. And in the fluid world, you don't know anything other than what currently exists, and that's OK. None of us knows what we're doing. We just didn't want to admit it, and we don't need to know anymore. "Knowing" your long-term life arc is not strategic, and it doesn't serve you. Worse, pretending to know limits the pace of your learning and the scope of your vision. Accepting that you don't know leverages fluidity and quiets the gnawing sense of inadequacy and fear. Disruption can genuinely become a feature, not a fault.

I'm in control *because I have a plan, an accepted degree, a good job with a great company, and I've invested my savings.* But you're no longer in control in the way that you think you should be. The variables today are vast and ever more beyond your control. And while that might strike fear in your adult heart, sit with the fear, and let yourself stretch out into the space that it provides you. Accept that the degrees you once thought were bulletproof are now vulnerable, the industries you thought were flourishing are now flatlining, the social institutions you thought would have your back have turned their backs.

Now what? What are you going to do about it? Will you get swallowed up by anxiety and overwhelm, or will you accept that control was always illusory, that the need to feel it in familiar ways kept you small and self-limiting?

The beautiful future that you think you can see clearly and navigate toward with the utmost control can disappear right in front of you. If you're not prepared, if you don't have options or an attitude and ability to create new ones, volatility will destroy you. True control isn't found in knowing all the outcomes and managing all the variables. It's found in managing your forward navigation without knowing exactly where you're headed. Remember, preparedness over predictability.

In the old logic of the fixed world, success was based on a series of logical and rational decisions to follow on paths that pointed most directly to financial gain and status. That's not what success is anymore. It can't be. The speed and scale of change preclude following old rational formulas. If you only play in the land of the known and familiar, if you never allow yourself to step into uncertainty, you will struggle to succeed over time.

Success is as much about what you know as how you keep finding your way through the unknowns and being ready to leap into the unrevealed. Some of your best decisions will be leaps of faith, incalculable risks.

Get used to not knowing how things will turn out, where you're heading in the long term, or what the future holds. Get used to the reality and experience of feeling "out of control," and experiment with how you hold that feeling, how you begin to discern when feeling out of control points to danger and when it's showing you opportunity. Open yourself to possibility instead of closing yourself off for certainty, because success is the exploration of the unknown; your need to know limits your ability to succeed in the fluid world. Stop focusing on preserving predictability when your attention should be on possibilities. Deal with discomfort, and figure out how to proceed.

Experiments to try:

- Move to a city or town where you sense community or opportunity.
- Learn a new skill that might be useful moving forward.

- Stop doing something before there's a clear next step.
- Make a small investment in a growth industry.
- Visit places that interest or excite you.

Your experiments keep your options open and continue to open more doors to learning and growth. Remember good life design combines what you want with what works. So your experiments will have to make sense for *your* real world: what you can afford, what you have time for, what you're resourced to support.

As you try these things, you're becoming an active learner. You're able to roll with the waves of change better and ease your need for control and certainty because you're confident in your ability to adapt and adjust as necessary.

Through experimentation, you foster three qualities critical for thriving in a disruptive world:

- curiosity—I *want* to try it.
- receptivity—I'm *ready* to try it (even if it's not familiar).
- adaptability—I'm ready to *learn* from it.

These qualities hone your preparedness for change because you're getting used to making changes and riding waves of change and disruption rather than holding on for dear life.

2. Make your best small bets.

Intentionally choose some experiments that serve as small bets on your ability to learn and grow, to thrive and succeed over time. Experiments that involve risk, a degree of uncertainty—otherwise, how else can you explore and grow? Make many bets, not just one or two where you go big and bet it all because you're desperate for change. String together hundreds of good small bets because doing so opens more space in your head and in your life than two big bets can. Keep investing in your loopy life and your need to avoid flatlining for too long.

A line with lots of little loops, lots of little experiments, on it is a life of continued adaptation and periodic redirection. You're not trying desperately to get unstuck and feeling uncomfortable doing it. You're not making high-risk changes to counteract the flatlining. Instead, you're continually growing and evolving through the phases of your life and the forces of change.

When you experiment, you no longer need to:

- cling to certainty or require certainty to act.
- tether yourself to the familiar because it's all you know.
- sacrifice your present happiness for some ideal future payoff.
- bet on the quality of the outcome because you invest in the quality of your choices.

The old logic said, "If I get an accounting degree, then I will have a smooth and secure career path. I can then go into cruise control and follow the path laid out in front of me."

The new logic of the fluid world asks, "What if I get an accounting degree?" and responds, "I could become an accountant, or a financial manager, or a teacher, or an entrepreneur. I'll see where skills and experiences take me in a changing world. Regardless, I believe in the value of the skills I'll learn, so I'll place the bet that they'll be useful to me moving forward."

Study accounting, or any other skill, because you want to, because you like it, or you think it's valuable, or you can see how it provides a core set of capabilities that you want to use going forward. But know why you're making that choice and believe in it, rather than making a choice because you think it will keep you safe and buy you security. It might. But that's not enough of a reason to do it.

Making good small bets means:

- dialing into what you want.
- accepting the risk and discomfort that come with not knowing outcomes.
- being ready to learn what the experiment teaches.
- asking questions about where the experiment can take you.
- looking around and planning for your next best experiment.

You're not investing in outcomes that you can't predict or control. You're investing in choices you want and trust to teach you something and take you somewhere.

You are driven to learn as an investment in an expansive future, not settling for a safe bet. There are no safe bets, only good ones based on the information at hand. Bets that build out your resource portfolio—that maybe provide long-term benefit or immediate pay off. Either way, you're spreading out not shrinking, becoming more resourceful and adaptive rather than rigid and afraid.

With this attitude and approach, you see yourself not as a fixed identity to which you must cling but as an evolving set of curated experiences and capabilities that will serve you over time.

3. Start with everyday experiments.

Start small, really small, stupid small. Start with tiny experiments that won't change your life but will build your ability to try new things, thrive in different contexts, and handle situations that may be anything from disorienting to difficult. Start with your current level of comfort and build from there, like exercising a muscle and watching yourself become more powerful. A new recipe. A different route to school. Buying a journal or sketchbook. A concert. Each a small stretch into the new and unfamiliar.

Be intentional about your everyday experiments, no matter how inconsequential they may feel. (They are anything but inconsequential.) The flaw of human growth and change is that we usually wait for big problems to motivate ourselves to do things differently: We set out to run a marathon without ever running a mile or try a high jump while standing still. Then, we're surprised when our actions don't have the life-changing impact we expect, surprised when we're too afraid to make changes at all. Intentional small experiments, like exercise, condition us for change: fitness, flexibility, speed, and strength.

Low-key forays into the new are a great way to build your preparedness and keep you alert and alive and ready for what's next. And small experiments are about agency: I can choose intentionally, differently—decisively. They're little power moves that nobody needs to know but you.

While you experiment, you create a portfolio of:

I-can moments, whether trying new foods, finding your way to or through a new place, or going somewhere by yourself or with new people. You're operating in figure-it-out mode, working out where you're getting lost. You're reading the instructions and deciding whether to follow them. You're admitting, "I don't know how to do this, but I'm trying to figure it out."

Get into this mode over and over because that's how you create forward motion and gain a palpable sense of moving through uncertainty, sensing small accomplishments, and tasting the sweetness of growth. You will find yourself thinking, "Yes! I can do it! What am I going to do next? And then?"

For-the-first-time moments to better understand what stimulates your nervous system, equipping it to navigate confusion, frustration, and fear. Get curious about how you react to and balance external direction with intuition and instinct.

I-did-it moments to seek out the right kinds of fear, the right challenges. Instead of contracting in the face of threat, you walk beside it. You come to realize that fear exists alongside action, not as a barrier to it. You need challenges to keep testing yourself and seeing what you can do. Facing ever-greater challenges means you keep discovering new levels of capability to continually feel alive and able. Every time you overcome a small fear, you get a large hit of "I did it!"

It-wasn't-that-bad moments in which you transformed gentle or acute discomfort borne of uncertainty and fear into intentional experiments to imagine your greatest pleasures. In those moments, you'll realize that you cannot feel totally alive to capability and possibility unless you are prepared to not only entertain but *welcome* feeling uneasy, anxious, afraid, or even a bit of pain. To unwind the cotton wool that muffles and mediates our most meaningful human experiences is to understand that things are seldom as bad as you thought they'd be.

I-loved-it moments, which build your desire for the next experiment. I call these *sjoe* moments, from the South African word for "wow," "yum," or "yes!" Design *sjoe* experiments into your life because the more you find yourself saying "I loved it!" the more desire you build to go find the next opportunity to experiment.

See all these as expanding your reference points and filling your portfolio of sensory-rich experiences. Stretch what's possible and desirable, what you can tolerate, and what you can enjoy. Give yourself more fuel, more fire, more to work with and play with.

YOU ALREADY KNOW THIS.

Think of your last trip to a new place, a time when you tried a new food or downloaded a new book. How did you feel? Alert? Alive? Awake? Present? Switched on? Dialed in?

Experimentation brings us into ourselves and into our world, and even when the experiments don't go well, we don't regret them. We remember them.

Keep creating those moments, even the tiniest ones, and trust that they're preparing you for more.

AVOID THIS: DOPAMINE CHASING.

It's easy to bounce around trying new things so much you never deepen your knowledge. However, your portfolio must be built. Your intention must be an investment in your capability and not just another hit of the new, because dopamine chasing is a type of rumination, and it will get you stuck. Don't do stuck.

- 5 -

FEEL YOUR WAY

Old logic: Brains rule!

New logic: Your best life relies on your body.

Your body was never supposed to be a part of your success story in the fixed world of rational choices that everybody recognized. With every year we grew older, we switched off our bodies, cut "knowing" off at the neck, and carried on. But those old ways of navigating life no longer serve us. It's time to reknit our knowing from head to toe.

Success has always been seen as a brainy exercise of accumulating and applying knowledge, passing tests, and getting grades and promotions. The body's always been treated as a hotbed of irrational feelings and risky longings that led you astray from your safe and secure path—a distraction from or a threat to success.

In this chaotic and fluid world, your brain's not enough to get you where you need to go. Your body will help you transform the Unraveling to the Renaissance, helping you to take all your fear, anxiety, and disorientation and turn them toward discovery and creativity. Your body will give you permission.

You have a deep know-how stored in your cells. Neither mystical nor new age, your body's knowledge is simply sensorial, instinctive intelligence common among humans and all the other animals that walk this earth. All your hard-earned wisdom sits alongside your agency and authority—that green light of action—in your belly and bones and heart and gut. Your fear—the stomach-clenching panic that grips you when you're facing a new challenge, not progressing the way you expected, or having to step onto paths that don't have a clear destination—lives there too.

Your body might want to stop you from being willful or experimenting or stepping out of your comfort zone by telling you that wherever you are is the only safe place to be. Instead, view your body as the compass guiding you toward the most foreign and fun and fulfilling territory in your life: the places calling you to explore.

When you start to use your body more, when you become more fluent in your body's language, you start to take yourself to the places you really want to go. Ignore your body, and it'll hold you back. Listen to it, and it'll take you farther than you thought you were allowed to go. You give yourself permission to explore.

NEW LOGIC IN REAL LIFE

1. Your brain might be a big problem.

Consider whether the brain you've come to believe is your trusted guide is still up to the job, especially when it is:

Overworked and overwhelmed from trying to make sense of how to live your life in the fluid world. Processing all your information and options tires your brain, and it becomes alarmed when it can't tell true from false or right from wrong. Juggling messaging apps and newsfeeds, meeting requests and passwords, is weary work that taps out the brain and inclines you to choose the path of least resistance.

A prediction machine, hardwired to protect you during high-alert days. Given the scale and nature of change, it's doing its work well and trying to recognize safety from among the options available to you. Your brain will always want to reach for the predictable and familiar. It will want to default to the known. In trying to protect you, your brain might turn you back too soon or stop you before you even get started. Unable to make sense of what's immediately around you, it might tell you to return to the base of your status quo.

Intellect alone can be self-limiting and works best in the land of the known when today you need to be increasingly comfortable in the unknown. If you rely solely on your brain to make your choices, you might keep making the same ones and feel frightened of choices that sit at the edge of the rational and familiar. You may become hesitant, reluctant, or slow to react. You might become so cautious that you miss out on all the juicy opportunities around the edges of your everyday.

Chances are, some of your best bets are buried underneath promises from your brain that it knows better. Desire is often hidden behind rationality. Risk-readiness gets muzzled by the logic of caution. Following the way is a brainy job, but finding your way is a job for the body.

Does that mean you don't use your brain at all? Of course not. The way forward blends and balances brain and body by combining the information available with your innate sense of direction and gathering all the best data you can while listening to your body. You learn what your body is trying to tell you by getting into conversation with it. When it's afraid, anxious, and sensing threats, you listen to determine whether those threats are discomforts or actual danger, whether your racing heart is a sign to run away or toward, whether your goosebumps are warning or welcoming. File that information and refer to it as you go.

Giving self-permission to feel your way doesn't dismiss or ignore your rationality; it brings more data into the mix, and there's a lot of untapped data throughout your body. Feeling your way also gives your brain a break.

The 21st-century adult can be plagued by overthinking. Drop out of your brain and into your body to tap the resources available to you there. Call upon your deeper knowing when you don't know what to do.

2. Think more gutsy, less brainy.

It's time to call upon your guts, your instincts, for guidance because in some cases, your gut knows better than your brain ever could. Gutsy can be synonymous with jumping off literal cliffs with a parachute attached to your back, but it also means being willing to do anything you haven't done before, anything you're not sure you can do. In times of stress or uncertainty, your brain will usually give up before your body will.

Your guts are the key to your growth and capabilities, to navigating the never-seen and never-done-before, to fixing things when there isn't a manual, to persisting when it's hard, to improvising when a solution isn't obvious. Gutsy is what this world needs you to be now. Not a superhero, but gutsy enough to contend with novel people and problems and to create new ways of working when the old ways don't work anymore.

Learning to listen to your instincts while you engage with your emotions unlocks so much space, giving your life room to stretch out, offering dimensions and perspectives you never used to think were allowed. You were too afraid to go there . . . but maybe your body can steer you wherever "there" is. You'll start to pay attention to what your instincts tell you. You'll start to engage with your emotional reactions to the unfamiliar while fine-tuning your threat-detection system to help you distinguish genuine danger from run-of-the-mill discomfort. When you need to stay safe and when you can head toward your frontiers.

When making choices or trying to figure our way forward, we normally start with our heads and maybe work our way down to our hearts. You will not think your way to your best possible life. You've got to feel your way there through the gut, which means we have three sources of information to work with:

- **gut:** deep steer (what do I know?)
- **heart:** emotional guide (what do I feel?)
- **brain:** fact checker (what do I think?)

When the path is clear and the information is abundant, start with your head and work your way down. But when there's an absence of information or experience to guide you, start in your stomach and move up through your heart and brain because each organ has a role to play in driving your way forward.

Integrated intelligence blends the best of all that is already known and your unique knowledge to help you make better and bolder decisions, but it takes permission: permission to listen to your body, permission to trust that integrated intelligence even if you can't point to it, to back your own wisdom as valid—even when it's not verifiable with facts or documents, even if it wouldn't hold up in court, or even if you can't explain or justify it to others. Remember, you're the authority in you, and you owe no explanations for listening to your instincts. Permitting yourself to believe in your own wisdom is critical to claiming your personal authority.

Can you permit yourself to believe that the best advice is your own? Permit yourself to believe that you are your own best leader?

By listening in to your intuition and instinct, you dial in to your personal value and wisdom. You combine how it's always been done with how *you* do it, combine the known with your unique consciousness, your practical knowledge and skill with your specific feel for something. *Your* way doesn't have to be the best way, but it is yours, borne of your life and your wisdom.

Perhaps you feel the word "wisdom" doesn't apply to you because wisdom is a white-haired thing. You haven't lived enough or know enough to be wise. But you *are* wise. Every human, regardless of age or experience, possesses some form of wisdom worthy of attention and respect. Everyone possesses wisdom borne of every experience they've ever had. You've been accumulating knowledge every day of your life, and the more intentional you become about that collection process, about the interpretation and use of all the wisdom, the farther you'll go and the happier you'll be on a journey that will rarely feel smooth or predictable.

3. Whole-body intelligence trumps artificial intelligence.

In a world of deep panic about whether, how, and to what extent our human intelligence will be replicated and surpassed by artificial intelligence, your bodily intelligence is one thing that can neither be replaced nor manufactured. *You* cannot be replaced. What you know, feel, and sense cannot be reproduced.

Your stored bodily intelligence is mighty, and if it feels too "out there" to imagine it as your guide, then see your body as your own best supercomputer, one nobody else has, one that only you know how to use best, one that cannot be replicated. Your value and relevance are amplified in and through your body.

To nurture that intelligence and fully tap the power of that supercomputer, you must act intentionally, pay attention to your environment, and pay attention to your body.

Your job is to be the most intentional data collector and processor you can be, to feed that computer of yours as much as you can as you set out into the exciting frontiers of your life. Optimize your real-time information-gathering and sense-making capacities, mining each new step for all the data you can glean. Particularly in times of uncertainty, you must rely heavily on real-time data to navigate new surroundings. To learn and adapt quickly, you must be tuned into the environment and how others are moving through it.

The more you pay attention to your environment, the more information you collect, the more you can work with, and the quicker you can learn. But you must be alive and alert to your environment, rather than allowing it to whiz past to get to the next meeting, activity, or goal. Remember that the world is a one-dimensional studio backdrop but a vast source of information. Collecting that information through the built-in power of your senses is how you dial into and dial up all that natural intelligence. Pay attention to your changing environments and to how you experience them: See, smell, taste, hear, touch as much as you can, and savor it because it all serves you. You store sensory experience as intelligence.

Exercise your senses like you would the rest of your body, consciously experiencing different contexts, becoming acutely attuned to the fluid world. You will:

- **see** specific colors and shapes.
- **smell** coffee, curry, roses, and petrichor.
- **listen** to birds, dogs, trains, and thunder.
- **taste** foods that are hot and sweet and new.
- **touch** textures, pick up snow, and stroke the grass.

The more you pay attention to your body, the more you learn how you react in different environments, how you cope with stress, physical and mental strain, excitement, confusion, curve balls, stumbles, and surprises. You may build body awareness by:

- noticing sensations and listening to what the head, heart, and gut are saying.
- knitting together sensation, emotion, and cognition.
- doing three-part body scans (head, heart, and gut) to check in before small and big decisions and noticing shifts and patterns.

We exercise intuition and gain greater connection to and understanding of it when we deliberately put ourselves in places where we need it: the unfamiliar. You don't really need intuition when you know what you're doing, when data and information can be your guide, when your rational self has so much to draw from. And you can exercise your intuition by simply taking a walk in a new part of town or along an unmarked path. You don't need to be far from home or facing danger to know your body. In safe environments, you can play with intuition, test its utility as a guide.

YOU ALREADY KNOW THIS.

You regularly use bodily intelligence in two commonplace ways: sense of direction (your compass) and reading a room (your intuition). How many times have you felt a tingle, a shiver, or maybe goosebumps that were inexplicable but impossible to deny? We often dismiss them when we need to listen in to them. Pay attention to those signals that are like a voice whispering to you when you just don't know the way.

You know there's a kind of intelligence that serves you when you don't know your way—a product of having found your way a thousand times. You just didn't think it was valid as a life guide. Don't complicate or exoticize body knowledge. You already have it. You've just got to dial in to it and use it more.

AVOID THIS: NAVEL-GAZING.

Don't get so wrapped up in yourself that you lose sight of the world around you. Yes, it's critical that you become attuned to your own body and what it's trying to teach or tell you, but make sure you're regularly looking up. You don't want self-awareness to tip over into self-obsession or for listening in to become listening to yourself alone. Your body is only as useful as it allows you to navigate this world in the most fulfilling way, so treat your investment in connecting to yourself as your greatest investment in community and human connection. Avoid navel-gazing because it will get you stuck. Don't do stuck.

- 6 -

FORGET ABOUT THE FUTURE

Old logic: Chase the payoff.

New logic: Invest in the present.

You've probably been asked about your future for as long as you can remember: *Who do you want to be when you grow up?* Your imprinted story says your current life is only useful as a pathway to a brighter future. But what if a future fixation doesn't work as well in a fluid world? What if the present is more valuable than you think?

You don't know what your future will look like—what the world will look like. None of us does. We never have. The future has only ever been an idea. An idea we felt comfortable and confident playing around with and predicting, assuming it would be a faster, slicker version of today. Now? With the scale and velocity of innovation and change, the future's anybody's guess, the predictions ever flimsier and more fantasy-like.

Unpredictability is the source of so much of the stress: the unraveling of predictable futures, the life blood of our existential Unraveling. Many people find it hard to pluck Renaissance out of uncertainty, though uncertainty is the source of rebirths.

Accepting that the future will only ever be an idea isn't a bad thing. Maybe it's the very thing you need to free up your best offers. Maybe it doesn't need to leave you anxious and untethered but rather excited, available, and prepared. Free agency, preparedness, experimentation, feeling your way, and intuition come into play when you stop using a shiny and predictable future as your aim and start building out a beautiful present.

Give yourself permission to forget about the idea of a crystal-clear future with a fixed path; accept, even embrace, unpredictability. Stop pretending predictability should drive your decisions, and free yourself up to find rather than follow, to design rather than default, to explore and create.

When you pull your exclusive focus away from an imagined future, you can invest in your present, not as submission to the chaos, but as a tactical grounding in what you can know and control: this moment. Invest in the quality of your now, rather than the potential of your future, to crack open your options. Here's how.

NEW LOGIC IN REAL LIFE

1. Work with the unpredictability rather than worrying about it.

When you treat unpredictability as a feature, not a bug, then the lack of clear paths opens possibilities rather than laying down obstacles.

By letting go of the need to know, you remain open to the emergent, not attached to the predicted. You'll either fixate on what you know or flounder in what you don't. You can't see the future clearly.

Development and disruption are too quick for anyone to have any kind of clarity. Lack of clarity can either leave you paralyzed and uncertain about how to act or lead you to look for familiarity amongst the uncertainty. Your aim is not to lock into what you think you know or to give in to either false predictions or paralyzing fear. You must find the most fertile space in between.

Aim to work with the future as it emerges by engaging with uncertainty, not by layering it with what feels like certainty, making false predictions, or succumbing to feeling lost. In the fixed world, focusing on the future meant you were one step ahead, but in the fluid world, focusing on the future can leave you lagging. Think inductive, not deductive. Be willing to set out without the clear map, accept what you don't know, and work with what you do.

In the old logic of the fixed world, you were laser focused on your future vision and treated the present as a pathway, which led to obsessing over years while losing sight of the days. The new logic of the fluid world urges you to focus on the present as a building block for an unknowable future, which means investing in your days to build out your years. Design your way forward from your present location rather than deducing it from wherever it is you want to go. Rather than lose sight of what lies in the distance—foolish in a disruptive world—work with the idea of a foreground and a background: Where do you *focus* your attention, and what do you keep in *frame*?

Of course, you can combine shorter and longer timeframes, blending front-of-mind activity with back-of-mind awareness. But keep the present in the front, the future in the back.

When you're highly invested in the present and generally aware of the future, focused on the next best options while maintaining a general grasp of your intended future, you're keeping track of trends and developments as they unfold while more closely focusing on:

- **feeding your sense of satisfaction**, happiness, and well-being.
- **learning** skills that might help you prepare for the emerging future.
- **adapting continuously through periodic changes** to prepare you for the emerging future.
- **feeding your energy and driving your curiosity** for what interests and excites you.
- **building your portfolio of experiences and capabilities** that might serve you as you and the world evolve.

Through your investment in the present, you're nimble, alert, and alive, which frees you up to:

- dream bigger, because you're allowed to.
- act faster, because you're not fixed in place.
- update yourself regularly as a work in progress.
- not know, but persist with confidence and curiosity.
- remain open and optimistic (not naïve) and full of anticipation.

Prize—if not prioritize—your current happiness and satisfaction, which act as fuel, fire, and kindling for your agency and desire.

2. "Numb" is your enemy—"happy" is your friend.

Your job as an adult is to keep yourself alive, not just with food and drink and shelter but with experiences, learning, and connections. Alive to what's in front of you, to what's out there. To what's emerging, to what's next. To what feeds you and what teaches you because the best form of preparedness in a disruptive world is feeling as alive and alert as possible to what's changing all around you. Happy people grow and learn, react and respond, faster than the grumpy and stuck.

Adults are expected to become numb after their teenage years or their twenties, when experimentation is tolerated, if not actively encouraged. They're expected to switch to autopilot, get on the routines-and-duties treadmill, and not ask too many questions about paying the bills. Becoming numb is meant to be what *good* looks like: ease, familiarity, stability, and predictability. That your days become a blur is meant to be the cost of being a grownup.

Nobody really wants to feel numb, but many don't recognize numbness as the natural result of a hugely predictable and routine life. A core unspoken—but totally understood—concept of adult life is that you're supposed to sacrifice today to pay for tomorrow, trade satisfaction for success and security because personal satisfaction and growth are nice-to-haves not must-haves; success is equivalent to satisfaction. In the fixed world, your number-one job is to secure a steady income. Everything else is secondary. But sleepwalking through life to chase material possessions and a shiny and secure tomorrow hollows out your days.

- You get *lonely* or lack a sense of strong connections because relationships and community aren't a priority.

- You become *self-obsessed* in that individualistic shiny striver's story, so you spend a lot of time in your own thoughts and head.
- You have *few interests* because leisure isn't valued, and free time is for recovery so you can work again.
- You have *little imagination* because you're so narrowly focused on working your way to a shiny future, you don't look up or around at what's out there.

When it's time to deal with or make your own change, you're too tired, uninspired, bored, or lonely to figure out what you want, what your options are, and how to go about finding them. You sacrifice today's satisfaction for success and security tomorrow.

Being numb in a fluid world is a liability. It means you're unresponsive, ill-prepared, and dialed down to what's right around you, numb to the possibilities of an uncertain but expansive future. You lose the capabilities to keep exploring and adapting and to correct your course as you and your world change. Your job in an unpredictable world—perhaps your job in life—is to stay alert and responsive.

Transform your new-world operating model: Invest in the quality of today to nurture an expansive tomorrow because investing in your present-day satisfaction isn't a luxury. It's how you become your most successful free agent, how you create your own Renaissance.

Starting satisfied and switched on means you'll move faster and learn more, be more daring and creative, and be more receptive to the new. You'll be more responsive for the simple reason that you aren't numb, that it doesn't take ages for shifts in the landscape to reach you because you're tuned in, laser focused on the world of ideas, relationships, experiences, and environments; you're choosing life every day and keeping your mind engaged, your senses occupied, your heart enlivened.

Will your life be easy? No.

Will you always feel happy? No.

Will everything go your way? No.

But maybe that's radicality: Switched off and living easy isn't the point; being alive and present, feeling stimulated and connected, is the point.

3. From Striving to Savoring

And now it's time to skewer striving. Striving! The default operating mode of any successful person, the way you work toward all the status you're meant to crave.

Striving is the source of much misery and grinding dissatisfaction because its starting point is discontentment with the present tense, a never-enoughness, a what-about-moreness. The striving worldview always puts the desired thing off in the distance; satisfaction is the reward for getting there: the next promotion, the bigger house, the flashy car.

You're meant to spend the prime years of your life chasing something more, which de facto means spending the prime years of your life dissatisfied with what is—until satisfaction itself becomes an idea rather than a lived experience.

Savoring means delighting, lingering, never wanting it to end because it's so good. Greedy, right? By the old logic of the fixed world, serious-minded, successful adults aren't meant to savor.

Zoom out. See savoring through a life lens prizing inputs as much as—maybe more than—outputs. Invest attention, energy, and interest in current experiences rather than banking on what they might buy you later. Savor powerful exchanges and experiences that stimulate, energize, and inspire—ones that enliven your sense of agency and allow you to move forward from wherever you are. Invest in your current satisfaction, your current happiness, as a strategic investment in your future success because if you set up a thousand satisfied days, you'll feel like your life was a success. And you'll be well positioned to grow and change in a fluid world.

Savoring takes life in, eats it up, loves what's right in front of you. You're not lying back and soaking in the beauty of an experience; you're not stumbling over what you're doing to get to somewhere else; you're not sticking around miserably because you believe it'll buy you something. You're actively and intentionally mining an experience for everything that feeds and stimulates you. Savor learning, enjoying, creating, loving. What do they tell you about yourself and the world? Spit out what saps you or feels like spinning. Don't stay in places or with people that don't help you grow or learn, where you don't feel connected and interested.

Reimagine a life more concerned with savoring days instead of sacrificing your days for years. Focus on feeding yourself through experiences here and now that are your fuel, your power, and your nourishment to keep going and growing in a world that needs you to do both for a long time. When you accept that your future is necessarily unknowable—and that unknowability is a good thing—savoring can start to feel more strategic, like:

- Being an excited history major rather than a bored economics major. Love your degree or professional development path, and trust that the passion and care you feel for the subject will help you build your portfolio. Be alive to what development teaches you beyond the curriculum and who you meet along the way. When the time comes to think about what's next, you'll understand your next best options and where and how far experience can take you.
- Taking the job that will teach you the most, connect you to the most interesting people or experiences, and represent the stretchiest next step even if it doesn't pay you the most. If you're clear about why you want the job and if you're committed to learning from it, it can't help but advance you.

Your most strategic investment in your future is making sure your now keeps taking you farther and wider than you can see from where you stand. Because by the time you've hollowed out today to pay for tomorrow, the road back to what matters is painful.

YOU ALREADY KNOW THIS.

Feeling alive is your biggest asset. When you're in a good relationship, doing work you love, and in a place that stimulates and excites you, you're more hopeful and powerful. You learn quicker, dream bigger, decide faster. Optimism—that sunny expansiveness we started off with—is born of rich days and dies in hollowed-out years.

Give yourself all the permission you need to create a beautiful now, and imagine thousands of beautiful nows adding up to your one beautiful future.

AVOID THIS: GRANULARITY.

In the fast-paced world, there's a risk of being so focused on what's in front of you that you miss what's coming. Tunnel vision isn't the intent here. And accepting what you don't know doesn't mean avoiding the reality of it; it means keeping an eye on it, getting to know as much as you can about where you expect things to head. It means looking up and down, zooming in and out, finding and not just following, which is a process of looking out and looking in, foreground and background.

To forget the future is to stop *fixating* on it at the expense of the present. Keep both the present and future in your sights at all times. Focus on your next best options while maintaining a general grasp of your intended future because granularity may get you stuck. Don't do stuck.

- 7 -

THINK SMALL

Old logic: A big life needs big plans.

New logic: The biggest lives might require the smallest steps.

In our imprinted success stories, bigger is always better: Go big or go home! Think big! All the best plans are *big*. The best lives are *big*. "Big" is synonymous with aspiration, smarts, and the ability to see beyond—better than the rest. And there's a lot of pressure to come up with big plans for a big life as a sign of your big ambition and talent—your pathway to the big job and the big house and the shiniest version of the person your aunt and uncle will respect the most. You bought security by aiming to be the biggest, shiniest version of the person everyone already knows with a career they can easily recognize and categorize. Bigness is a net positive.

Is it?

Maybe, just maybe, in this unpredictable world with its unknowable future, you can give yourself permission to back away from all the bigness. At the least, you're not required to assume that your biggest, best life needs big-sounding plans and ambitions to make it happen. Grant self-permission to believe it's OK if you don't have big plans. Maybe you don't need them to be successful or to feel like you're on the path to success. In fact, maybe it's better if you don't have big plans.

As a free agent in a disruptive world, it's time to embrace thinking small, not to dim your ambition but to keep progressing until the time is right to dial things up.

Finding your unique way, rather than following a default way, is inherently a small-steps approach. You become action oriented and focused on quality next steps: quality learning, quality experience, quality information gathering. You're neither timidly tiptoeing to the next safe space nor autopiloting your way to the vision you think will save or serve you. Instead, you're all eyes and ears, engaging with the world around you, no matter how far you can or cannot see.

Thinking small is companion to forgetting about the future—the action-oriented, adaptive, and curious way that you move forward when you're not fixated on reaching a predetermined destination. What might that look like?

NEW LOGIC IN REAL LIFE

1. Small attention meets big intention.

First off, let's distinguish thinking small from small thinking:

- **Small thinking:** limited imagination and ambition; narrow; myopic

- **Thinking small:** tactical execution and exploration toward the big and unknowable

Thinking small isn't about having a small and safe life. Instead, it's about having a life in which you are allowed to spread out, grow, and evolve. And in a fluid world, the best way to do that is, maybe counterintuitively, to think small because the biggest, rangiest dreams need the smallest steps to tap into your inner explorer for discovery.

The beauty of thinking small is that you move gradually toward things you can't fully see or explain. You're off the hook for knowing exactly where you're going or what to expect along the way. You get to try things out without feeling like you're a deviant or a deadbeat. You let your explorer lead without worrying you're going to get into trouble, firing up your agency with each small step.

Is going astray about thinking small? Yeah, it probably is. Your learning loops are likely paved with tiny forays into the new that may grow bigger or bolder as you can see more clearly. Your small bets are small. Your next best option might be the smallest step.

Along the way, your path gets wider. You do a little more wandering because you don't have the whole path mapped out. You don't need a map, and maybe you don't want one because you want to remain open to what might happen. Along the way, you work with your own capabilities, letting them emerge and evolve, alongside the world's possibilities.

Many people believe they've got their futures sketched out and so promptly start sleepwalking toward their desired destinations, like airport travelers riding those moving walkways to their gates. They've got it all worked out: They just need to get there. But you don't have it worked out. You can't! And that's OK.

You're going to loosen your grip on your need for big plans and instead focus on bold intentions because working with intentions over plans is central to self-permission, where you claim a little more space to adapt, evolve, and create by accepting the inductive, evolutionary nature of your life. Think of intentions as a general direction rather than a precise destination and replace detailed plans with bold intentions and see what you may be free to do.

A *destination mindset* locks you in tunnel vision as you strive to get wherever you think you want to go, while ignoring whatever you might see, learn, or experience along the way.

A *direction mindset* sets out in a certain way but remains open to changing direction based on what each step teaches and tells you. The direction mindset:

- reminds you that you can be deliberate about your aims without being certain of how they'll play out.
- recognizes that you have no idea what you'll discover in the days ahead, and your intention is to remain responsive and adaptive to what you're learning.
- keeps your options open by not attaching your sense of security or identity to any specific outcome.
- blends knowing with not knowing and lets you leverage the best of your current information with the possibilities of the unknown.

You can use *the background/foreground* approach again here: Your intentions sit at the back of your mind, animate your decisions, and inspire your sense of possibility. They are a source of energy and velocity.

Your attention on the other hand—eyes, nose, mouth, ears—stays focused on the steps ahead, where you'll unlock your real value and the fullest possibility of the moment. When you're on the verge of something truly big in your life, you can't see it clearly from where you're standing. And whatever you think you can see from where you are is probably not the fullest, clearest sense of how far you can go. You've got to step toward it, into it, to discover what it is.

Treat thinking small as a kind of under-the-radar advancement that steers you to the next spot from which you can reassess what you know and what you want. Build your portfolio deliberately, place small bets, keep your senses open to interesting tangents, meet new people, grow your network, gain new insights, develop skills, feed your senses, loosen your limitations, and have fun. All of these are catalytic steps forward that give new information and offer you more perspective.

Whether you're clear about what lies ahead for you or you're sweating and stumbling as the world shouts options at you, stash your intentions in your back pocket along with your permission slips. Know both are there, guiding you. Take them out and look at them as you move forward and learn more about yourself and the world. Be prepared to change things up or throw things out as you keep granting self-permission to go ever wider. See the path forward as expanding to places that may look scary from where you're sitting because you haven't stepped into them yet, which may look like:

- getting midway through the first year of an accounting degree you thought you had to obtain only to realize accounting doesn't work for you and changing majors.

- signing up for a course without being sure how you'll best use it.
- leaving the "dream job" for something that better serves you.
- exploring a new venture without a clear plan or map.

Thinking small is nimble, agile, responsive, and thoroughly unstuck. It's action oriented—doing one thing and then the next thing—because you know that each experience or action taken will give you feedback while pushing you forward. Thinking small is also relative and personal. You'll have to interpret how it works for you, depending upon your clarity and the nature and number of your options.

If you're completely at sea, start with what's right in front of you. Navigate through a compact set of "yes" and "no" questions: This thing? Or that thing?

Slightly longer line of sight? Stretch out your sense of "next" to months instead of moments. Don't force yourself to think in years yet, but get a feel for just how far ahead you can and want to see.

Instead of trying to map your career, focus on one good next choice to maximize your growth and learning and keep you building toward bigness. Regardless of how granular or grand your "next" might be, you are stepping into and stopping with it: What can this choice teach me? Where can it take me next?

Allow yourself to expand and contract based on the clarity and space you have in which to explore, as well as your willingness and ability to invest in a course of action. Stretch out when you feel safe to do so, and pull back when you're moving through uncertain territory. All the while . . .

2. Keep your locus of control tight.

The biggest danger in a fluid world is losing your sense of control, feeling lost, and not knowing where to go next. It's easy to feel overwhelmed by possibilities and choices and retreat into the familiarity of the known before you allow yourself to advance. The more you embrace possibility in the fluid world, the more you might feel pushed and pulled by forces beyond your control. Thinking small tells you to keep your locus of control tight to build up trust that you have the capability to deal with whatever comes next.

Think of what it's like being in a new city or exploring streets you don't know. You instinctively draw in, don't you? You keep your possessions close and minimize distractions and variables. You become hyperaware of the next left or right, of the landmarks and the signposts. It's no different when you're moving to or through new territory in your life. You want to pull that control into yourself to avoid feeling lost or overwhelmed. At the same time, you enjoy the discovery of new sights and sounds and experiences.

The aim of thinking small is to manage risk while maximizing learning, and in thinking small, you'll avoid doomsday scenarios and the paralyzing grip of what-if panic. From my own experience of traveling the world, I know that when I stayed calm, focused, and attentive, I always found my way through the most complex projects or the most confusing cities. Through thinking small, you'll do two critical things:

1. When life is deeply uncertain, you'll tell yourself it's OK to keep tight and small as you move through new parts of your life, treating your step-by-step process as a strategy rather

than a deficiency, accepting the experience and leveraging the learning.

2. Over time, you'll grant more and more self-permission to go into new spaces because you'll gain confidence in your own authority to find your way through the thicket of the new and the tough. You'll build discomfort tolerance by racking up I-did-it moments.

Your tight locus of control unlocks your agency. Instead of whirling from endless outside forces, you act and respond with tight choices that don't extend your risk or responsibility beyond what you can handle. Energized and alert to what's next, you can make more informed choices and feel comfortable with those at every step.

Confusion doesn't have to blow up into catastrophe; nervousness doesn't have to translate to paralysis. When you have big dreams and plans, you can avoid the risk and anxiety of overwhelm by breaking down that bigness into small, manageable, and strategic steps.

You lower the stakes and lower your temperature. Granting self-permission to think differently about what it's going to feel like to keep growing up—that it won't all be smooth and seamless and planned out years in advance—and that's OK. It's more than OK. Thinking small is how to operate if you want a truly big life on your own terms, and you can begin by:

- scheduling regular check-ins with yourself to see what needs adjustment.
- keeping your timeframes shorter when you need to make tactical progress.
- building a close network of trustworthy guides.

- refusing to overextend yourself financially through small bets.
- starting something even when you can't see it fully.
- stopping something that was supposed to be great.
- avoiding the approval-seeking overshare when you're feeling uncertain.

Small steps, not always forward but always heading out, will teach you something every step of the way.

3. Think different rather than big.

Disruptive technologies and a digital world are inviting us to extend our imaginations beyond the old-logic notion that bigger is better and move toward novel possibilities and never-done-before options. Uniqueness has as much pull as bigness now—maybe more?—which means thinking beyond replication toward invention. Breakthrough thinking isn't just about the breadth of the plan or the dream, but its unique utility and take on whatever already exists or must exist.

Thinking small liberates you to do or be *abnormal, weird.* Big plans are often hugely conservative because they can only ever reflect an outsized version of today's version of the status quo. They're built on certainty and predictability, and it's difficult to extract anything truly original from that.

Uncovering the unique, extracting the weird, and leveraging the new might involve two key things:

1. **Dot connecting**

Connecting dots is critical when you're focused on creating something novel in relation to what already exists or will exist soon: new applications for old things, updated versions of existing things. Thinking small makes dot connecting easier because you're taking small steps forward deliberately while remaining alert and knitting together as you go, connecting people, ideas, and industries. What do they share? How might they resonate? How could they learn with or from each other? Remaining open and adaptive to new connections and applications is critical to looking for small experiments and bets and next best options: Try this here, open that there.

2. **Ditching elevator pitches (until you're ready)**

When you're thinking small and different, permit yourself to be speechless. The more you take small steps toward something that's new to you, the less you might be able to describe it, fully or fluidly. Invention doesn't always come with an elevator pitch—at least not immediately. Having big words to match big ideas is not required for your thing to have a life. You're allowed to keep it close until you're ready, allowed for it all to feel less slick or smooth than what you'd imagined.

Invention isn't always immediately recognizable, and that's OK. What's recognizable can be overrated at the outset. A little opaqueness means there's still much to be revealed. These aren't problems necessitating a halt to progress. Hold the discomfort of unfamiliarity long enough to create something new and different, and put it into the world.

As you design your big, beautiful life, you must be willing to not know how to describe what you're creating or the clearest path to get there. You do not need an elevator pitch to justify action! It's not a flaw or sign of failing. Trust that you're onto something, learning something, on your way somewhere—even if you can't see the destination. And it doesn't need to be articulated until you're ready.

YOU ALREADY KNOW THIS.

Some of your most exciting experiences have required the smallest steps: the new cities you've visited; your first days on a new campus or in a new building; that sense of excitement as you took single steps into the spaces that were calling you. You knew you were excited, intent, aware—and a little bit (but not terribly) scared.

Learning and creating new things is a step-by-step process. You've built with LEGOs, learned an instrument, and adjusted recipes. You know these processes of discovery are about building capability and stoking imagination one step at a time.

Apply the same fluid-thinking logic to your own life, and understand that is it not a liability to lack knowledge of where exactly something will end.

AVOID THIS: DOING IT ALL ALONE.

Taking small steps might mean needing help, advice, and directions. Because you won't know where you're going, you'll find yourself in unfamiliar territory without a long line of sight, which can feel scary, lonely, and disorienting, like standing on a busy street with no idea where to turn next. The greatest gift in that situation is the person who comes along and points you in the right direction when you ask—the kindly stranger, the good Samaritan.

You're not rewarded for doing life alone, and there's nothing heroic about a solitary journey. People rarely achieve great things in isolation. Ask for directions, desire company, hold a hand, ride the slipstream behind someone else if you're tired, seek out a kindred spirit. Those who default to isolation may become stuck. Don't do stuck.

- 8 -

TRAVEL LIGHT

Old logic: Accumulation buys you security.

New logic: Flexibility is the new security.

You've been sold the lie that ownership is a requirement of adulthood—that growing up and old is a process of steady, gradual accumulation: of power, of responsibility, of stuff. You're supposed to want it all and want more of it all the time. Maybe it's time to confront the reality that generating and servicing more—treating "more" as a requirement of adulthood and a prerequisite for success—has become increasingly impossible and even less desirable. Maybe the ability to travel light *is* more.

Maybe you're feeling pressure now to have more, to prove that you're going to make or own more. After all, you're only truly treated like a grownup when you have certain things: the first car, first apartment. The earlier you get them, the more impressive an adult you are. The bigger they are, the brighter your future.

Maybe right now, you're looking at your parents' house and feeling like you won't ever walk through a similar door or looking around at what you have and feeling an aching not-enoughness. Or maybe you're looking at your future and thinking you don't want all of that—you want less or, at least, your own version of more. But there's a shame attached to that, isn't there? What's wrong with you? How can you lack the ambition or desire to not want more? The concept of more drives so much "supposed to" and "should" that it keeps you stuck in a prescribed life script, afraid to write for yourself.

Accumulation might have served us in a fixed world, where stockpiling stuff served as protection: lords and their manors, queens and their castles. But a fluid world doesn't enable accumulation like the fixed world did, and it doesn't support accumulation for accumulation's sake either because everything gets moved around, taken away. It's harder to swim when you're weighed down.

Allow yourself to entertain the idea that you don't *have* to have more, that you don't have to want the old version of moreness, that you don't have to accept that not wanting more all the time makes you unambitious, that not having more doesn't make you a loser. Allow yourself to ask what you truly need and want to navigate adult life today, not as one-off philosophical questions but as practical questions to ask yourself over and over again.

The fluid world gives you space to address the unspoken but obvious reality that the quest for more of everything can weigh you down. While accumulation was seen as power in the fixed world, it might sap your power to evolve, adapt, and reinvent in this fluid world. You're allowed—even required—to design a life of traveling light and see where it takes you.

NEW LOGIC IN REAL LIFE

1. Take only what you can carry.

Whenever I think of the difference between being an adult today versus being an adult twenty or thirty years ago, I can't help but imagine a road trip.

Adult life used to be a lot like a road trip in a gas-guzzler down interstate highways with a clear destination in mind. You knew where you were going and how to get there, and you went with a take-all-you-can-carry and are-we-there-yet? mindset to go along with it. Optimizing for comfort made sense. Of course, you took everything as long as it didn't spoil your trip or stop you from getting where you wanted to go. You didn't need to worry about what you threw in the back seat or the trunk because your weight or agility didn't matter.

Accumulation makes sense in times of stability and predictability, but limiting your mobility and flexibility at a time of rapid, high-volume change might no longer be your best life strategy. When you want to protect optionality, you need to be prepared to grow. The heaviness of assets makes you expensive, uncompetitive, unlikely to pivot, and rocked by reversals.

Traveling through adult life today, down all its winding paths through unfamiliar towns, means acknowledging you can't pack for every scenario. So you take only what you can carry. On a hiking trip through the mountains, you're light and carrying everything on your back. On a plane trip to a new location, you might stick with a carry-on bag to minimize variables and maximize pleasure and ease. The more exotic the trip, the less you must drag with you. The bigger the adventure, the less you want to be weighed down.

Assets can narrow your adult path. This isn't news, and it's not controversial—it's precisely the point. Assets have always shaped your path by providing roots and grounding to place or to position, which is perfect for certain periods or points in your life but can be a liability in times of high uncertainty or peak accelerated growth. As you design rather than default, being intentional about accumulation and ownership means being aware of how grounded you want to be, the scope and scale of your ideal flexibility and optionality.

Much of today's adulting angst centers on accumulation, the deep fear that you're not good enough because either you don't have enough or what you have isn't good enough. The questioning of worth usually has less to do with character or talent than with assets and accounts. It's the vicious treadmill of keeping up, the spiraling self-loathing if you're not. The rising expectations of ownership can lock you into supporting your lifestyle and lock you out of evolving at pace because so much seems impossible, rogue, and reckless when you've got debts to pay and a lifestyle to support. Being willful, going astray, undertaking experiments, and making small bets all start to feel impossible when your priority is lifestyle.

When you take only what you can carry, you grant self-permission to ask, "What do I want to carry now? At this stage of my life?" You don't have to default to the assumption that you want to accumulate or that success means you must. Taking only what you can carry gives you permission to decide what *you* want. Using desire as your driver, you intentionally design a lifestyle that adapts as you evolve, which will shift and change according to the times of your life and whether you're cycling quickly through the new, digging deep into the ground, or preparing for one or the other.

What you can carry will be a function of your professional and personal life, your mental health, your support networks, your sense of connection to place or people. Ask yourself how much you *want* to carry, and don't judge yourself if the answer is *not much*.

Presumably, you want and need more grounding as you get older, create family, deepen roots. That's the expected trajectory, but it need not be yours. Thriving adults aren't only the ones with big houses; they're also the ones moving as lightly as they want to through lives they love. Even as you build family and home, you get to decide what that looks like, whether your design includes a house with a yard, a flat with a nearby park, or a home on wheels that travels with you.

Remember, designing your life is where functionality meets beauty. It's where your life is purposeful and pleasurable. So design the life that has the lightness you can and want to manage.

You get to:

- define value in your own terms.
- pick things up and put them down.
- deny material accumulation as the metric of success throughout your life.
- decide what *you* want at different stages of your life and adapt accordingly.

You get to stop, to shed, to get sleeker. You're not denying yourself or becoming a monk. You're figuring out how you move best to and through different phases of your life, which might mean letting things go, giving things up, and reprioritizing.

Radical, right? Old people can downsize, but everyone else is supposed to upsize all the way. Maybe upsizing will work for you. Maybe it won't. Either way, entertain your options, and allow yourself to believe that accumulation isn't the only one. Explore the experience of lightness and what it would take for you to feel it.

2. Treat velocity as a priority.

Your biggest danger as an adult is getting stuck in one place, overburdened and out of choices. Inertia is your enemy. Getting unstuck is hard. You must always have forward motion on your mind, even when it feels like you're settling into a life of steady accumulation. You must be ready and able to move, even in small steps, to oil your responsiveness for adaptation and growth.

Forward motion might require you to stay light-footed when you launch something new or need to take a leap. It may mean managing big changes with minimal risk. You might make an investment in your long-term growth, like going back to school to extend your knowledge or diverge into something new. However volatile your context, make sure that you're prepared to move, which isn't easy when the priority is protecting accumulation. Any one of the inertia-breaking decisions—to speed up? to slow down? to pause?—will likely feel too risky. Any sign that you aren't forward marching through more-more-more can feel like a sign of weakness.

In the old logic of the fixed world, there was an unspoken rule that adults must prioritize accumulation over velocity, flexibility, or adaptability. In a fluid world, though, you must treat velocity as a priority so you don't find yourself in a place you can't get out of, a place lacking options, or a place without the ability to make the choices you want because it would threaten your apparent success.

When the market is turbulent, investors unload, keep their options open, move toward safer bets.

In the new logic approach to accumulation, liquidity is protection, and you may manage your portfolio of experiences and skills to keep your life liquid, to accumulate only when the conditions are right, while keeping your locus of control tight. There's wisdom in making decisions in a volatile marketplace that simultaneously protect you and maximize your growth. You don't have to stay liquid forever, but be intentional about what you buy and what you let go.

It sounds like common sense, but when you've been trained to accept the idea of steady, gradual accumulation as the hallmark of victory, staying loose and liquid sounds radical.

You are allowed to make yourself responsive and adaptive to changing circumstances. It doesn't make you weak; it makes you strategic. This fluid world enables and rewards fluidity in ways that were unthinkable decades ago:

- **Fractional roles:** With the rise of small and solo businesses, more small companies and individuals are looking for people to fill fractional roles.
- **Shared use and ownership:** Rideshares make car ownership unnecessary in many places; accommodation shares make property ownership less necessary than it used to be. People can now explore options for shared use or ownership that make living light easier.
- **Lateral moves and career descents:** People are deciding they don't want to keep accumulating more duty and responsibility. They're deciding that the forward march to the corner office isn't what it's cracked up to be.

- **Downsizing:** You don't have to wait until the kids leave home. You can decide at any time that you no longer want or need what you have.

In the name of striving for more, many people gut their personal lives, hollow out their relationships, and contract their lives into a narrow pursuit for the next shiny thing. You get to decide what *more* means to you: more time with the people you love, more leisure to pursue your broader passions, more opportunity to engage with the wider world. In a lighter, looser, more liquid life, redefining *more* may free you up to invest in experiences rather than material possessions. When you have less to lose and less to lug around, you'll encounter more opportunities to place small bets on yourself because often, *having* more stops you from *being* more and *experiencing* more.

3. Balance accumulation with autonomy.

Over the last decade, we've seen ever-greater value placed on autonomy and independence, flexibility, and freedom—reflections of growing individualism and reclamation of individual power in a fluid world. Individualism is an assertion of authority over your life and work. People are beginning to ask what they're willing to give up or give into to achieve success, like chaining oneself to a desk or sacrificing a rich life to be rich. And you can follow that path if you want to, but you don't have to. The answer is less important than the willingness to ask the question. It's permission, not dogma.

Increasingly amidst the Unraveling, people are valuing autonomy as their primary marker of success. If the institutions aren't going to take care of them, then they'll damn well assert their authority to take care of themselves, look after themselves, choose how they live their lives. Ask questions about what you want to accumulate, and at what cost, to claim your authority to arrive at your own decisions without fear or shame, and design with boldness. It's the ultimate flex.

Time replaces money as the currency that marks your success and power. Autonomy becomes a form of agency, a tight locus of control that lets you maneuver as best you can so that what you have enhances your life rather than blocking you from doing what you want.

Claiming autonomy doesn't mean going it alone. You can prioritize family, leisure, and community as you build a rich life or become materially rich. Claiming autonomy means claiming your inherent ability to make choices that suit *you* and *your* story.

Adult life doesn't have to be a collection of dictated responsibilities. You're allowed the freedom of choice to design a life that hints at adventure, pleasure, meaning, and joy. Valuing and claiming autonomy means you don't have to work for someone else the rest of your life or work in the same way your whole life.

Consider the implications of traveling light to:

- **put down** what doesn't suit you anymore, whether relationships, goods, or responsibilities.
- **pick up** what you deeply want and say "yes!" to that which lights you up, moving through life like a treasure hunter on the lookout for beauty and wonder and delicious singularity.
- **keep your hands free** for new beginnings and new endings.

Traveling light isn't about deprivation. You're not trying to be a monk (unless becoming a monk is part of your loopy life design, of course). When you make yourself lean, sleek, streamlined, alive, and alert, you are claiming your autonomy. You're not losing out on *anything*. You're gaining free agency.

You're the ultimate autonomous individual, able to make choices about your time, values, priorities, and relationships. You adapt to a fluid and ever-changing marketplace.

YOU ALREADY KNOW THIS.

The idiom "you can't take it with you" may be the truest cliché ever!

If you've lost anyone in your life to death, you know that what you came in with is what you leave with. We arrive on Earth with nothing, and we leave with nothing. Material accumulation serves only the most temporary needs. There is no biological imperative around it and no existential requirement. In fact, the existential requirement is precisely the opposite: Exist on this planet with the lightest of steps so the comings and goings bring less friction.

AVOID THIS: UNTETHERING.

Not feeling connected or grounded to anything, lacking a sense of people and place, can be disorienting. Traveling light doesn't require a lack of connection or community. Instead, it frees you up to deepen your connections to place and people, to invest in relationships and connection, and to spread out as needed into new places when the time is right or change imminent. Traveling light isn't about drifting, becoming nomadic, or failing to prize what builds your base. It's you deciding what your base looks like and how it evolves over time, how much of it is vested in what you *buy* versus what you *create.*

Connections are the most critical things you can accumulate. There's security in high-quality relationships, success in the quality of your experiences. The most successful people aren't the ones with the biggest houses but are those whose lives spread out the farthest or whose love runs deepest. Untethering and losing all sense of connection can quickly get you stuck. Don't do stuck.

- 9 -

LOOK FOR TROUBLE

Old logic: Avoid trouble if you want to succeed.

New logic: Go toward trouble to thrive.

Good boys and girls avoid trouble, and you've avoided trouble because you're afraid of getting into trouble. It's time you stop avoiding the trouble and step toward it, not to find a fight but to find a teacher.

You're meant to avoid trouble as you glide with glacial ease toward the alleged ideal life an adult can find. Along the way, you subtly shift toward a stay-in-your-lane mentality that means not looking around or out at the world beyond your profession and acquire a keep-your-head-down attitude that shuns speaking up or out. You make yourself small and safe and stay exactly where you're supposed to.

Small and safe and in-your-lane worked in the fixed world where trouble threatened to rock your foundations. You plugged into a ready-made role and played the same role over and over, order and predictability your top prize. But now that you must thrive in fluidity—to rely ever more on your individual agency to navigate instability—you must step toward the trouble instead. The more you avoid trouble, the more you avoid innovation, possibility, connection, and meaning. You avoid growing and making your best contribution to the world. Avoiding confusion and discomfort means avoiding learning how to thrive in a volatile world.

These *Ten Permissions* could all be about making life less difficult, about easing the struggle of adulting, but we're living in a world full of trouble. It's time to make trouble your friend.

Grant self-permission to go toward that which is hard or hairy, toward problems that persist or mysteries that intrigue. Permit yourself to imagine that your aim in life isn't to go to sleep but to stay animated, invested, and alive. When you look for trouble, you are out in the world and unafraid to engage, no matter how unexpected, unknown, or gnarly it turns out to be.

Instead of staying safe and sensible, which you're mostly advised to do, go looking for trouble to discover the very best parts of what you have to offer and even what the world offers to you.

NEW LOGIC IN REAL LIFE

1. Don't design an easy life.

While it's not necessary to manufacture a hard life or seek out suffering to give life meaning, you must accept that some struggles bring the best of you to the surface. Easy isn't your friend in a fluid world.

Yes, you can and should experience ease, flow, and comfort as you navigate your way forward, but ease cannot mean editing out all forms of friction and fight, all the difficulties of life, and whatever you think you're going to dread. While ease can be a feature of your life, an easy life isn't ideal.

Avoiding trouble—problems, challenges, setbacks, struggles—doesn't serve anyone in a fluid world. All the capabilities you need to adapt, evolve, and grow accelerate and intensify when you step toward hard things. Grant self-permission to rise to the hard things and so rise with them.

Consistently avoiding trouble intensifies navel-gazing, and your personal struggles become oversized. The slightest wobble sends you searching for a label and a diagnosis. At the first sign of struggle, you might even panic and wonder what's wrong with you because everyone else has fancy holidays and happy families. Irritation is soon treated as pathology. Confusion is a good reason to give up or turn back.

When you become addicted to an easy life, you:

- have no tolerance for discomfort, no ability to absorb friction.
- don't know how to advocate for yourself (or anyone else).
- become disconnected, unmotivated, and brittle.
- grow numb.
- get stuck.

People usually get stuck not because their lives are too hard but because they're too easy. Ease breeds fragility, complacency—a dullness that doesn't shine up. Ease breeds little of the fire and desire that creates velocity, which is why so many of the easiest lives can quickly feel like they're going nowhere.

When you shift your focus from personal ease to personal growth, you start believing that the calculus of your decisions doesn't surround what's easiest or most expeditious but also what stimulates your growth and the satisfaction you gain from learning. From there, you grant yourself permission to take things on, look for challenges, and stretch out toward learning, not just compensation and rewards.

You permit yourself to ask:

- In what issues do I want to become involved?
- About what ideas or fields am I passionate?
- What potential innovations inspire me?
- What problems do I want to solve?

When you're out there looking for trouble by asking these questions, think local and think global—problems the whole world is talking about, problems that maybe nobody else cares about, and all the problems in between. Noticing, innovating, and solving are critical for free agents whose roles are to add value to different situations throughout the courses of their lives and careers. As a free agent, your focus is on invention and value, not bringing more of the same, not bringing more of the *safe*.

Easy made sense when you were executing, when application and repetition were key. But when your focus is invention, looking for hard challenges for adaptation and growth is key. Desire, remember, is the driver of your greatest learning and your best experiences. Looking for the issues or ideas that matter to you—that you want to dig into—will keep raising your personal bar.

Call looking for trouble a growth hack. See it as a shortcut to personal growth in the 21st century. Valuing struggle is not only a contribution to your ability to continually evolve but also a service to the world. Seeking trouble instead of dodging it makes you a highly valuable contributor.

2. Give a shit about something.

Caring about something just doesn't cut it; I want you to *give a shit* about something as a key part of your success story.

When I was growing up, the people who gave a shit weren't successful. Successful people didn't give a shit—not any kind of shit at all—because giving a shit distracted from making money and getting ahead. Giving a shit couldn't be monetized, and companies hadn't taken a liking to shit-giving, but those days are on their way out. What you care about—your values, what you value, how you offer value—matters.

Knowing what you care about deeply is about finding, not following. By knowing your values and value, you discover your right fit, where and how you want to and can contribute. It's you standing out rather than fitting in, and it's where you get to stand for something that matters to you, whether that's health care or the arts.

Free agents decide what to contribute, and giving a shit puts a megaphone in front of your yeses and nos, gives clarity, provides velocity, and amplifies your intention while supercharging your will. In a fluid, troubling world, giving a shit does the magic job of locating you within yourself and the world at the same time, crystallizing that sweet spot where your talents and interests and values intersect, the point at which you'll apply your intention and agency.

Am I telling you to go find some global fight between good and evil? No. But I'm encouraging you to find something you're curious about, passionate even; something you care about and believe in, as well as in your power and ability to contribute to the kind of world you want to live in. A world that isn't a backdrop for your individual success but a place where you can make your greatest contributions among a collective of people striving for something better.

For better or for worse, trouble wakes you up and brings you to life because you either must fight for it or find meaning in it. Caring—*giving a shit*—will bring you to life. So:

- find a problem and solve it.
- find a community and join it.
- find an issue and learn about it.

Look for the parts of your world ripe for reimagining and set your talents on them. Unleash your talents on the problems that keep you awake at night—climate change, inequality, and access to the best possible social services—and on the local problems that the world doesn't know about but which matter to you. In your community, church, office, or even your home.

A new world needs imaginative solutions, fresh voices, different perspectives for collective thriving. As you look for things to be about, be driven by your:

- **values:** issues that spark your sense of right and wrong, good and bad.
- **know-how:** stuff you know how to do better than others.
- **curiosity:** stuff that drives your interest.

And accept that:

- it's going to be hard, and that's a good thing.
- it's going to take time, so don't lose heart.

Looking for trouble takes a lot of permission because quick and easy has become the norm; when something is hard and takes long, you may wonder whether it's right or if it's worth it. You're supposed to want an Amazon Prime kind of life—order and get—but *giving a shit* isn't about cheap and quick. It's about investing time and resources into creating things that matter to you and to the world.

Go to the things that people are struggling with. Not so you alone can fix them or be the hero of the story, but to learn with and from others about what it takes to do hard things, have hard conversations, dig into hard challenges, and spend days, weeks, or months trying, just trying. Learning to be patient and persistent—to linger, to let things unfold—is a superpower in the fluid world, and you get to see all that hardness, all that trying, as the sign of a successful life. You also get to be part of a community of give-a-shitters.

When you figure out what matters to you, you'll naturally meet other people who feel the same way. You'll connect through shared interests and passions and the desire to make a shared contribution.

While success has always been individual—me, myself, and I—and we've got the loneliness and burnout stats to show for it—looking to the world and how to add your best value places you within something bigger. The new metric of the fluid world becomes contribution rather than achievement; success is something hard that was made, built, done, or created. It took time and was for something other than yourself.

3. Trouble is your best teacher.

Trouble teaches you because trouble is hard and complex, the answers aren't obvious, and nobody can agree on them. You've got to linger in not knowing, persist through confusion. And, yes, potentially be tested by failure. Everything that made you avoid trouble is expressly why you must move toward it. Actively move toward the places where challenges and curiosity meet because in those places, you learn:

- **problem-solving,** a critical skill in a fluid world. Figuring things out and finding new ways forward are skills people need, skills that are invaluable to you as a free agent. You can't learn those skills existing in stable, seamless situations. Your biggest payoffs come from being a part of solving someone's problems. Shift your mindset radically from "stay in my lane to avoid the hard stuff" to "go find hard stuff because it'll teach and reward me."
- **invention and innovation.** Trouble signals opportunity and innovation, and part of your strategy as a free agent isn't to look for what's solved and sorted; your strategy is to look for opportunities. Trouble is where the opportunity for innovation is ripe, where humans experiment for solutions. Learning how to think differently, share risky ideas, and collaborate in creative design are golden skills in a volatile world.
- **empathy and engagement.** When you set out to tackle something tough, you begin education in human behavior, and you need that education more than ever, you need empathy more than ever, in a highly individualistic world

> where understanding and appreciating the unique and the weird is no longer an afterthought. Digging into the hard stuff means dialing up your empathy and curiosity, and your ability to ask questions for connection and understanding: Why is this happening? Why does it work that way? Can it work better?

As a free agent, you're looking for the spaces where you can learn and contribute, connect to like-minded people, and create things that matter to your clients and to the world. Treat part of good life design as designing something that matters to somebody beyond yourself, not in some grand, Earth-changing way necessarily, but in a way that sparks your mind and your interests, your agency, and your talent. Your sense of contribution.

Combining stuff you're good at with stuff you care about creates the very best in life design. While you won't be able to operate from within that perfect Venn diagram intersection all the time, savor it when you can. When something that matters meets your greatest gifts, there is magic.

YOU ALREADY KNOW THIS.

You're alive and animated when involved in things you care about, be they stray dogs, arts and culture, or teaching kids soccer. But feeling animated and alive wasn't part of the old-logic equation, so you're not sure if you're allowed to treat your passions as priorities or if they have to sit on the edges of your life, edges that get narrower and narrower with age and responsibility. You're worried that being animated and alive might lead you away from success and security, but they won't. Being alive means caring—*giving a shit*, feeling, trying, experimenting. Dreaming.

AVOID THIS: CHRONIC ANGER.

Trouble can annoy, frustrate, and disappoint. It can highlight the best and underline the worst in people. It can inspire hope and deepen pessimism. Avoiding trouble is avoiding all the highs and lows of getting involved with the tough stuff. So you must be prepared to feel more without your big feelings becoming a new problem. Negative emotions must not consume or define you. Trouble must drive your desire to engage with the world, not push you further from it. Becoming trapped in chronic anger is becoming stuck. Don't do stuck.

- 10 -

MAKE BELIEVE

Old logic: Creativity isn't a pathway to success.

New logic: Creating is your primary pathway to success.

We're living through one of the most creative times in human history, quite the proclamation when everyday news stories are about the sky falling, the robots coming. Your creativity is needed—your unique and uniquely human ability to generate the new ever more required and ever more permitted. Allow yourself to bring it to the 21st-century Renaissance party.

Artificial intelligence is changing the face of work and the role and function of human labor, liberating humans from repetition and routine. Any process or function that can be replicated soon will be done by computers. Repeatedly executing on a predictable set of commands is becoming robot, not human, work. Everyone, from programmers to lawyers to graphic designers, is facing a kind of existential crisis: What can I add if robots can do everything?

Depending on where you stand on the matter, robots either pull the rug out from under you or force you to pull out your magic carpet. Artificial intelligence is nailing shut the coffin of industrial-era mentality, though, of course, not of industry. Things will still need to be made.

What will the humans make?

How will humans contribute uniquely to what the robots are doing for us?

This chaotic world is also a deeply creative one; the chaos invites creativity, calls out for it. This world has problems—big ones—calling for creative solutions. Major industries—health care, insurance, banking—are evolving rapidly to keep up with an evolving world. The very nature and scale of the disruption mean we've got to be ready to remake and reimagine on a routine basis.

Deep down, you may not be sure you are creative—that you can create, that you're up to the task of driving the change and not just responding to it. Maybe you were told or decided a long time ago that you're not "the creative type." Or perhaps the old logic still lingering in your worldview can't quite see how creativity is a legitimate pathway to success.

It's time to reframe your relationship to creativity, to treat the act of creating not as the work of a few talented elites but as a fundamental human capability. In a world begging for your most unique, useful creative contributions, grant self-permission to offer your creativity.

NEW LOGIC IN REAL LIFE

1. Seize your creative free agency.

Most unsettling about the rise of artificial intelligence, the velocity of change, and its impact on work is that success all along has meant behaving kind of like a robot: Do the same thing over and over; don't stop; have few feelings and even fewer needs; respond to commands without asking questions.

The concept of work has always been vaguely robotic, and we were rewarded for our most mechanical forms of productivity. Originality, emotion, and creation were never words you could associate with corporate success. What new era of human labor are we entering when being robotic isn't as valued or valuable as it used to be? Why have human robots when you can have real ones?

We're being called upon to show up and share value differently, to distinguish what makes us valuable. All the originality, emotion, and creativity once deemed distractions are becoming desirable. *Repetition is giving way to creation, uniformity to uniqueness.*

Industrial mentality didn't welcome your personal flair or unique contributions because those things got in the way of execution and repetition; they were an inconvenience to profit making. Creativity was the enemy of predictability, and if you wanted a "real" job, you had to ignore the restless, uncontained energy difficult to wrestle into a cubicle or corner office or factory floor. The people who had permission to create were the artists, the elites. Everyone else satisfied themselves with the routine productivity bound up by a 9-to-5 schedule. Workers neither got to be creative, nor did they need to be.

More than ever, we've got to see ourselves as creative free agents who bring unique and necessary contributions to each new role, project, or assignment, which requires all kinds of self-permissions to access your creative capabilities and instincts, trust them, share them, and believe they're a valid and valuable contribution to your work and to the world. We get to play now, and we must if we believe we can make things we believe in. We must improvise and mess around in ways that are uniquely human because that's how we give ourselves permission to thrive in a world where being machine-like is no longer the best strategy.

You are no longer a replication machine. You are a creative free agent. And you need to design your life around free agency.

Create instead of being creative.

Creativity is your ability to bring something new into the world, which is less about drawing and singing and painting and more about imagining an old thing done in a new way or imagining a whole new thing all together. Creativity unlocks your (you guessed it) agency! Anticipating, problem-solving, experimenting, adapting—all are ways to create something that doesn't yet exist, no matter how small. Dialing down your creative capabilities means dialing down your agency. It's time to dial it back up now.

Considering themselves "creatives" makes many people uncomfortable, but acknowledging that they can make things? That's a core aspect of being human.

In real life, creative free agency looks like:

- designing new services or approaches.
- finding new ways of working together.
- refreshing existing offers.

- updating old approaches.
- launching new products.
- fixing niggling problems.

Creative free agency can be done inside the same company as more organizations evolve into responsive marketplaces of needs and services. It can be done within your industry or field as you manage a portfolio of clients or roles, even across fields or industries if you're connecting dots. Creative free agency means you're *responsive* to a clear and felt need for a specific kind of service or support. You're working with a marketplace where you can *add and create value*. Which takes you back to shared value, to contributing to processes and experiences that meet a clearly felt need, that respond to a specific challenge, or that enable growth and expansion over time.

Creative free agency is as much an attitude as a way of navigating your career, wherein you're able to evolve and continually add value. Your expectations and attitude aren't only shaped around doing and delivering the same service or support every day or every year, but also evolving and adapting to continually create and recreate to keep pace with the demands of a changing world.

Distinguish the intentional collection and exercising of creative capabilities and sensibilities, your "I can" from your core "I am" professional identity. Intentionally build your portfolio of creative capacities relevant to your chosen field without necessarily seeing yourself as a capital-*C* Creator or "Creative."

Tap into all the things that weren't allowed in the office, all the juicy human stuff that kept you or keeps you from being robotically productive:

- **emotional intelligence** to consider how people will act and react in response to something
- **empathy and curiosity** to understand how humans behave and what works for them
- **boldness** to stretch out what you think is possible or desirable

The irony? Lean hard into your humanity to be more useful than the robots. You must, which runs counter to every old-logic script running in your head about who you're allowed to be and what you're supposed to do. You must unlock and unleash the most human parts of yourself that allow for collaboration and creation.

2. More DJ, Less DaVinci

"Creativity" has always sounded so lofty and outsized: If it wasn't in the service of generating something new and majestic, then what was the point?

Most people feel intimidated when trying to create something from scratch, but if you skip the DaVinci mindset, you can use a disc jockey—the modern DJ—as inspiration.

The role of the DJ has evolved and adapted to become ever more creative, making new songs in the process of spinning old ones. Mixing and mastering links and connections between songs or styles, taking recognizable songs and giving them unique spins. DJs create fresh new music out of songs that already exist, and the lived experience is something that's delightfully recognizable and refreshed at the same time.

By leaning into your DJ mindset, you own that to be creative *also* is to:

- update and upcycle.
- remake, retool, and reinterpret.
- consider what's possible and try it.

Your ability to generate new ideas, interpretations, and inspirations is creative work, which is easier than ever when gaming, social media, and entertainment shape your life, when you've got software to help you make things and you don't have to start from scratch. Give people something that they want and need. Find your offer, find your audience. Teachers. Finance people. Hairstylists. It's never been easier to bring your unique voice, experience, and perspective to your field and to the world through household applications that platform your ability to make stuff from presentations to posts to podcasts.

Podcasts! The perfect example of 21st-century make-believe, an explosion of opinions and ideas, where people play with silly constructs and niche concepts. Some are hosted by famous names, but the vast majority are created by people who have a specific interest or focus. People who *give a shit* about something.

Every industry in the world is ripe for reimagination or reinterpretation to greater or lesser degrees. Each is already evolving at pace and contending, as I write this, with the implications of artificial intelligence: Education, health care, banking, and insurance are four familiar industries begging for 21st-century updates—how kids get educated, what the buildings look like, whether there are office buildings at all, how you receive health advice, how you access your money. None of these industries are traditionally creative. Yet each must evolve and adapt profoundly in response to a changing world, and the changes must be driven by people willing to create something different from what already exists.

When you draw your inspiration from the DJ and not DaVinci, you give yourself permission to mix rather than make from scratch, to play with the best of what already is or things that are begging to be linked up or mashed up. A good DJ transforms an event and music by mixing, reinterpreting, and connecting existing music in new ways: Mix old and new; insert a fresh beat into the middle of an old song to give it a totally different spin; sample. Whatever your approach, give yourself permission to *reinterpret what already is* by slowing it down or speeding it up, changing some essential element of it so that it can serve a different purpose, *connecting dots* between industries or genres or styles.

You don't have to have the most original ideas, a wildly impressive vision, or deep training over many years to bring your own take to things. You don't have to start with a blank canvas. Whatever you make doesn't have to have a frame around it to be valuable.

3. Think pop-ups as well as permanence.

One of the great shifts over the past several decades has been the evolution of the DJ to an artist. DJs were always workmanlike—useful, but not artists per se. Art was a designation for the singers, the musicians, the people who created original music that lived forever. Now, DJs claim their places right next to other musical artists. Yet most DJing is about making things *that aren't permanent.*

In the old logic, building and creating were only useful if you built something "that would last." In the fixed world, the only reason to create was to make something of consequence or beauty that would stand out above the others. If you couldn't, there was little reason to try. But in the 21st century, for better or for worse, you're not limited to that which is permanent. You shouldn't be—there's a fundamental impermanence to this moment that's both unsettling and liberating, Unraveling and Renaissance.

This century is about creating what a unique set of people want and need in a moment, or for a period. We're putting things up and taking them down, leveraging intransience. We're creating things that meet specific needs, serve a niche purpose or a specific moment, and then retooling them for other uses. Bespoke offers for specific audiences.

Stadiums are being created for specific events. Restaurants service a season. Shops open only for Christmas. The current world supports and enables what is modular, on-demand forms of creating that don't come without cost or consequence but that do allow for a little more freedom to create things that don't have to—and maybe shouldn't—last forever.

If or when you have the opportunity and ability to create something of lasting value, then do so. Don't limit your imagination to believing that those creations with lasting value are the only creations that have value, though. What you make doesn't have to be your magnum opus, your place with a plaque on the outside. It just needs to be something you want to make and something other people want. That's the sweet spot again, where you start to make your best contributions, all of which take risk, vulnerability.

Sharing something new is inherently scary. You put a piece of yourself out into the world and wait to see what people think. You have had creativity drummed out of you because not being creative was "safer." This is especially true for men who have been taught that vulnerability is "girly" and creativity not commodifiable and for women who have been taught to avoid making waves. Instead of creating, they shut those parts of themselves down. Bringing their fullest human to work or to the world still feels dangerous.

Forget that old danger. It's boring, and the old logic doesn't serve you anymore. It's caveman stuff that puts all your value in myth and mysticism rather than reality. In fact, the reason there's so much Unraveling happening now is because this world is requiring us to be vulnerable and make waves. We get to—we've got to.

Inside, you may be worried that you'll be penalized if you show up as your fullest self, which—traditionally—isn't the pathway to success. It feels scary, hard. But you don't have to hide behind a desk anymore. Maybe you can't, and as liberating as that notion is, it's also daunting.

Maybe it felt easier to plug into a role and do the same thing every day. It's OK. I get it. Permission is not just individual; it's social. Not just for each of us to create our own things, but for all of us to create new ways of working, being, relating—together.

We allow ourselves and each other to:

- **work in drafts:** You won't get it right the first time, whatever it is, so don't judge the first draft so harshly that you don't carry on. Expect to work through multiple drafts of whatever you're creating to come to something that you want to put into the world.
- **not try to please everyone:** Ditch likability as your number-one aim—once you try to create something new, you have to accept it's not for everyone. Maybe *you're* not for everyone. Your job is to find the right fit, and if you can't find it, *when*

you can't find it, you look at yourself and what you've created with care and curiosity to work out how it, or you, needs to evolve to find your place in the world.

- **treat failures as iterations:** Your relationship to "failure" must shift if you're going to learn, adapt, and create. Every time something doesn't work out as you expected, you don't get the response you'd like, mine the experience for learning: What can each failed attempt teach you that will allow you to evolve and grow? When viewed this way, failures are but steps on the path to success.
- **ask for help:** Creation is not a solo job. The very best products, services, experiences, and ideas that you've had have been the product of a collection of people. Finding people to help is not some white-flag moment; it's an intentional part of creating the resource portfolio you need to keep creating over the course of your life: strategic, technical, visionary, and emotional sounding boards and collaborators with whom you consult over time. These are your people, and your people will evolve with and alongside you.
- **play:** Create space for you and your people to play, whether with pen and paper, a computer, or in the open air. Play can look like so many things, but enjoyment is a requirement, a lack of immediate purpose or output. Allow yourself to do something, try something, feel something without it having to result in an immediately useful outcome, and you'll feel good along the way.
- **stand out:** You're probably so conditioned to fit in, to not be seen as arrogant or attention-seeking, that putting what

you make into the world feels vulnerable and presumptuous. It's time to untangle shining and standing out from seeking to control, dominate, or demand. Because in the desperate effort to fit in, the world is losing out on so many of your best contributions. Social permission is a must to celebrate, rather than criticize, as a first instinct—to support and not judge as a default response. Take up space. Stretch out. Invite others in with you. There's no need for false hype or false praise, but you must be willing to create spaces for people to bring their best and then figure out if or where their bests fit.

YOU ALREADY KNOW THIS.

Creating is powerful and pleasurable. There was a time when you made stuff, mixed stuff up: sandcastles and dances and bike tracks and games; Pinterest boards; playlists. You made stuff and had fun doing it until you were told that making stuff and having fun weren't part of adulthood and put it all away.

Take it out! Look back to whatever you did before you turned twelve, and think about the parts of it that brought you pleasure. Let your younger self guide you in your process of permitting yourself to create, thus reacquainting yourself with your inner creator.

AVOID THIS: HIDING.

You can get caught up in the process of generating great ideas and beautiful content and keep it all to yourself. But there's no point creating if you're not going to share it with your world. Yes, it's risky, and it's vulnerable, and that's precisely why you can't keep your best contributions to yourself. Put what you love into the meeting, the conversation, the world. It'll be scary. You'll wish for just a moment that you hadn't. But then, then! No matter how it was received, you'll feel alive.

Believe you can make, and make what you believe in. Then, put your creation into the world to bring it to life. Creating without sharing is how creative people become stuck. Don't do stuck.

- Conclusion -

PERMISSION TO PLAY

Old logic: If you want to grow, blow up your life.

New logic: Stretch out one permission at a time.

I don't want you to reach the end of the tenth permission, put this book aside, and think, "Hmm . . . that was interesting." I don't want you to treat this book as another set of good ideas in a world awash with good ideas. It's not reflection I'm after but action. Because this book serves as your first permission slip, your first green light that whispers, "Go!" and says you can create the life you want on your own terms. If my mission is to encourage social script-flipping, then there's a latent script around how you make change in your life that's desperate for a 21st-century update.

Permission is inherently an active proposition, a catalyst to show up to the world differently as your whole and best self. It's not a meditation or an incantation; it's not even a good idea. Permission is a spark nudging you to engage with yourself and your world differently, telling you that you'll be safe enough when you do.

For me, "permission" recalls school field trips. Oh, how I loved field trips. Lining up to board the school bus with my packed lunch in hand, relaxing into my seat, giggling and chatting with my friends. I didn't care where we were going as long as we could explore the world and ditch the stifling routine for a day. To this day, I can still recall that sense of freedom, adventure, and excitement in my body. *That's* the energy I want you to carry into this.

What's your version of the field trip, your lived experience of feeling permitted to explore or experience beyond the familiar, expected, and routine? The trip, the day off, the night out? Feeling free, safe, and acceptable stepping into a space you want.

Don't *think* differently as a result of reading these *Ten Permissions*. Act differently. Live differently. Make different choices. And being different is, of course, the rub.

Making different life choices can feel difficult, even terrifying, particularly when your mind turns to your biggest choices, the help-me-I'm-stuck! areas of your life. We default to our familiar, conventional choices because making new ones feels too high stakes. I get it.

A career in social change taught me just how hard it is to make different choices even when the existing ones are painfully undesirable. It taught me that we need to think differently about how to go about making new life choices, how to think about human growth and change, with less of a focus on problem-solving and more on giving ourselves permission to play around.

Most people imagine having to blow up their existing lives to design a more desirable one, and most are understandably afraid of blowing up their lives even when they want to because they're too scared. Of course, they are. Our social default model treats change as:

- painful and serious.
- having a before and after.
- high stakes and big leaps.
- cognitive and introspective.

Quit your job! Go back to school! Move to a new city! It takes most people so long to make those kinds of choices that most never do. They accept their status quo and default stories because any out-of-the-ordinary or against-the-grain choices feel risky, too much like hard work—particularly now, in the Unraveling.

Who's got energy to design a new life? Who's going to entertain more challenges when the world is in a never-ending crisis? Who wants life to feel even more precarious? Nobody I know. So we sit in waiting, wanting to change but exhausted by the prospect, aware of the need for different lifestyles but overwhelmed by designing for ourselves.

We need a new approach to human growth and change, and that is why you must give yourself permission to approach life design differently and in a way that might feel counterintuitive. A way that's more patient and pragmatic, maybe even a little playful.

Play around with these *Ten Permissions*, not because you want to fix your life in the first go-round but because you're gradually stretching it out into new spaces. That's what permission allows you to do: Explore new spaces, take up more space, go into places physical or relational that otherwise felt off-limits, and give yourself permission to go there with a smile on your face and promise in your heart.

Treat self-permission as a gentle unfurling rather than an

all-or-nothing transformation. Find a spaciousness to your life choices and feel safe there, secure and confident in yourself as pathfinder and life designer.

As exploratory and nonlinear as your life will be, playing around with these *Ten Permissions* will feel just the same. Not linear, gradual, and cumulative, this wending process will gradually heighten your sense of agency and capability, your willingness to learn, experiment, and adapt.

Being playful doesn't mean that you're unserious or irrelevant; it means that you allow yourself, particularly at first, to focus on choices that are:

- small.
- low stakes.
- pleasurable.

I know, I know. Small, low stakes, and pleasurable are not the usual qualities of good boy or girl professional pursuits, not things you'd normally turn your attention to, but it's OK. I want you to start playing around with permissions and find your most appealing starting spot without all the blow-up-your-life consequence, to accept the radical proposition that designing the life you want means making many choices, many juicy small choices, not just a few big and painful ones.

Start to play around the low-stakes edges of your existing life, and permit yourself to find space there first. Allow your permissions to tap and leverage joy and pleasure. That's what permission is for. Nobody ever asks for permission for something they don't want, that doesn't feel good, that doesn't meet a need.

Maybe you'll feel irresponsible or indulgent entertaining joy—starting where it feels easiest—because serious adults are supposed to be nose down and output focused. But you're in the business of life design, not short-term fixes, and that requires a different kind of strategy. Thriving in the Unraveling means accessing positive feelings whenever and however you can.

Granting self-permission doesn't have to feel like hard work, and it can't feel too hard at the start. Otherwise, you won't do it. It's unsustainable.

Will you eventually want and need to take big leaps? Yes, probably. Will this feel hard at times? Of course. So make sure you're ready when you get there. Relax your brow. Soften your shoulders. Channel some proper permission energy to feel your way into free agency by tapping into your lived experience of *feeling* permitted.

For a lot of you, seeking permission will recall tension and fear because it was always asking an adult authority if you were allowed to do what you wanted. But you're not that kid anymore. You're the adult now. And you're the only authority whose permission you need.

Soften your pent-up fear of seeking permission and focus on having it, that sweet sensation of being able to play around in areas of your life that may seem unconventional or irrelevant, spaces you might resist because you'll worry they won't be "productive" or "effective."

Good! See this book and your decision-making as training for a lifetime of productivity reframing. Start to play around with permissions by focusing on your:

- body.

- leisure time.
- conversations.

YOUR BODY

Some of you might be squirming now: *Who talks about the body in a book like this?*

Change is a brainy set of good ideas. You sit and journal, reflect and plan. You make up your *mind* to change. No, you don't. I mean, you do, but your mind's only part of the equation, one that gets quickly overwhelmed by emotion and sensation and a lifetime of experience of feeling unsafe or unaccepted, which is why there's such a gap between awareness and action. People know what they want but don't act on it. Those default stories are sticky.

You can't *think* your way into feeling permitted. You must *act* your way there, one chosen action at a time. And to take action, you must feel safe doing so.

Safety lives in your body, not your brain. It's your body that'll hold you up with the fear and anxiety you've been storing in your cells ever since you were born. Granting self-permission will help you feel secure in doing the thing that might have previously made you feel unsafe.

Because permission lives in your body, you'll start to give it to yourself by dropping out of your head and into your body, the same body that's afraid, excited, anxious. Yes, you'll observe your thoughts, but you'll have to grapple with your feelings and sensations if you want to act differently.

Locate permission in your body: Experience permissions as feelings rather than ideas. How does it feel to experiment? Do small steps make you feel anxious? Keep track of your feelings; make notes on them.

When I sit down to create something, I feel . . .

Notice your sensations: When I take my life outside, does my heart start to race? Do I sweat? Start tuning into your belly, feeling around with what's buried and what's bubbling up.

If that feels woo-woo, understand that you're getting fluent in your own physical and emotional reaction to change, to trying new things, experimenting with other and new ways. The more fluent you are, the better you are at managing your complex set of reactions to designing your life. The more you tap into your body, the more you can work with it. The more you ignore it, the more it will trip you up.

Nothing connects you to your body and its reactions and sensations more than movement. Nothing switches on your agency more than making the decision to move your body.

Moving your body achieves three things:

- fires up your agency.
- creates awareness of your body, its sensations, and emotions.
- puts you out into the world, where you can play around with your permissions.

You cannot play around with permissions from an inactive and inert space, so if you find yourself lying on your bed thinking hard about permissions, it's probably time to get up and get moving. In deciding to walk, you get willful, go astray, take it outside, possibly experiment, probably forget about the future for a little while. If you make one tiny choice as a 21st-century grownup, make it the decision to walk down the road, up a mountain, to familiar places, or to foreign ones. You'll decide; your paths will evolve. Treat your walks as tiny field trips even if they're to the most familiar place. Show up to that place each new time you arrive. Walking is so ordinary that most output-oriented, productive adults overlook its power. Yet just making the decision to walk out the door is the simplest and most powerful articulation of choice and desire: Do I *want* to go? *Where* do I want to go?

Asking and answering those questions represent the subtlest shifts in self. You're driving. You're choosing to move and moving forward in a specific direction. Give yourself permission to take a walk as the simplest, humblest way to activate your body and agency and to play with permission. Then, keep doing it and come alive to your senses.

That's the shift, right? From dead-eyed walking along a familiar and predictable path to being alive and alert to your evolving surroundings, looking for opportunities, fully aware of what's changing.

A lot of adults see their senses go to sleep over their lifetimes. They power down their most basic abilities to interact with the world and exist in heavily routinized autopilot modes. Boost your adaptability and teachability by heightening your senses, coming alive to your environments, finding your way through your world and life with a heightened sense of what you're experiencing and learning.

Treat this as a chance to play around with taking it outside, experimenting, and feeling your way, to name a few permissions.

While you're on your walk, don't zone out. Instead, try to spot specific things, listen to birds, dogs, trains, thunder. Make it a game you play with yourself—a useful, albeit playful, game.

Observe how you feel your way through the experiments. If you try Vietnamese food and hate it, get curious about what you don't like. Then, try something else. Oil your agency; make yourself aware of choices, how you make them, and how you feel about them.

YOUR LEISURE TIME

Forget about work, family, or home, all the high-consequence spaces in your life. Instead, focus on your leisure time. Maybe you don't even recognize your leisure time, your sofa time, your after-work hours, that time you often fill without thinking. It's your permissions playground.

The Latin root of the word leisure is *licere*, meaning "to be allowed or permitted." Of course, leisure *is* permission. Its entire point is choosing to do something because you want to, allowing yourself to spend your time on things you choose. It's desire, not duty, which makes it hard for good adults to pay attention to, much less prioritize. In a world where your value is so tightly wrapped up with work, allowing yourself to pay attention to, to prioritize and play around with, your leisure time is your greatest permission.

Your free time isn't free; it's agency in action. Leisure is the perfect space to tone up desire through hundreds, even thousands, of choices that will have no grave consequence in your life and yet make up the substance of your life. Nobody has to know what you're doing on a Saturday afternoon. Nobody may even notice what you choose to do on a Sunday evening. But in making those choices, you start to experience the low-key empowerment of being everyday intentional, of starting to design your days, so that you can design your career and life.

Practice each of these *Ten Permissions* in your leisure time. Being willful, going astray, taking it outside, experimenting, feeling your way, forgetting about the future, thinking small, traveling light, looking for trouble, make believe! There isn't a single permission that you can't play with in your leisure time. So give yourself permission to play, a space that feels safe, easy (easier?!), and possibly pleasurable. Your insides might be screaming, "BUT! BUT! Leisure time is irrelevant!"

It isn't. It's the perfect safe space to start designing your life.

Every weekend, ask yourself what you want to do. At night, ask yourself what you want to eat. Play around with I-want Wednesdays or I-want weekends, when you get intentional about what you want to do.

Will you do everything you want to? No.

Will you get everything you want? Of course not.

But you'll start to tune into desire, express it, feel it as you navigate it from the inside out: What's hard for you? Where are the spaces where it feels easy?

Say the words "I want" to yourself and then to others: *I want Italian food tonight. I want to go out and listen to live music. I want to see my old friends Sally and Clarence.* Feel the energy that comes with saying what you want and acting on it, the immediate feedback you get from the action.

Does it feel scary to access your wants? To acknowledge and say them? A little fear is OK, but don't stop at fear. Get curious, be kind, start to work with your wants in a way that feels more aligned.

I know this is not what-do-I-want-to-be-when-I-grow-up territory. Don't worry! You're becoming a little more decisive and assertive, realizing perhaps that you have more choices than you'd imagined and that you're equipped to make them.

If all you want is pizza, then get curious about it—not judgy or critical, but curious: What does pizza do for me? Why do I like it so much? How does it make me feel?

Sound silly? Well, when it comes time to ask yourself what you want from a relationship or a job, you'll have yourself under an intense microscope, so get curious here now, when it doesn't seem to count. Care about yourself making small choices, and see how they offer insight into the bigger ones. The more self-awareness you build, the more agency you kindle.

Light up your agency with "yes" and "no," two small words with tremendous power. Yes is an invitation, an opening. No is your surest stop. Yes is a choice. No is a choice. Yes leads to action. No leads to action.

Become aware of how it feels for you to say "yes" or "no," to set those boundaries, and to give yourself that direction. Because saying, "No, I don't want pizza" is a helluva lot easier than saying, "No, I don't want to marry you." Spend all the time you need sharpening your boundaries on pizza so you're ready when it's time for proposals, or job prospects. Free agency requires next-level boundary-keeping, so get comfortable now.

Will you always be crystal clear in your "yes" or "no"? No, of course not. Sometimes you'll feel a very firm "maybe," or you'll feel nothing at all. That's OK.

Treat indecision as a reason to get curious rather than to switch off, a spur for you to design rather than default. Look closer. Decide what's getting in the way of your clarity. The more you light up your "yes" and "no," the more you feel like an actor, rather than feeling like you're being acted upon, handled. No longer victims of circumstance, you're an agent in your own narrative, a narrative scripted by many tiny yesses and nos you've probably become unaware of over the years.

Seek out beauty in your leisure time because it's the perfect way to practice being present, navigating from now, moving with intention from wherever you are. Natural beauty. Artistic beauty. Urban and rural, human-made and all-natural. The birds in your own back garden to the mountains or sea two hours away. A beautiful meal, a beautiful tree. Any beauty not bound to a screen or limited to an idea, a beauty that reminds you of being present to what's possible and desirable.

Again, it's hard to forget about the future in your office. The physical experience of being super calm and finding your way is hard to conjure unless you've put yourself into a beautiful space where there's nowhere else you need or want to be. Yes, it's a presence hack. Use it.

YOUR CONVERSATIONS

During times of change, you may want to sit in your head, even in your bed, to go inward, get reflective. But you must entertain a subtle dance between inward and outward, between your thoughts and feelings. At the end of the day, you must be ready to take action in the world, to put yourself into the world differently. And the best way to observe is with and through your conversations and making your permissions explicit, identifiable.

We ask for permission, so verbalizing who you are and what you want is critical. Now you're asking yourself for permission, but you still must put words to your wants.

See your conversations as little permission conduits. Observe them. Become aware of how you're showing up to them and how they're playing out. Notice your exchanges: what you want, what's at stake, and where the joy and fear sit. It's almost impossible to give yourself permission if you don't put words to it.

Do not be afraid to have the very first conversation with yourself: *Hey, Jillian, what are you so afraid of here?*

Remember the power of self-talk. Whisper if you must, make it as quiet as possible while you lay in bed at night. Still, state what you're afraid of, what you're excited about. Put your thoughts and feelings into words. See the translation of desires to words as an ongoing process of introspection and exploration, looking in and stepping out, stepping out then looking in again at what you're learning and how you're evolving and adapting as you go. Which desires spark panic in your system? What feels the most transgressive to say? Become more fluent in your desires, aware of what you feel and can or can't express, even to yourself.

When you're ready, state your desires to others—for the first time, or more regularly, or with more intent. Start small, start safe, and spread out as you go. Use the phrase "I want" routinely and intentionally to take the sting out of the conversation, to lower the temperature of it. Not because you'll always expect to get what you want but because you know you never will if you never say it.

Routinely stating your desires, starting with the low-consequence ones, helps you to engage with yourself and others more honestly, to create more mutually satisfying relationships, and to find more beneficial solutions. Stating your desires brings clarity about what you want, what you can create, and what you can't.

Join groups of people, whether around a table, on a museum tour, while reading books together, or while playing sports. Putting yourself in a group, whether formal or informal, means meeting strangers, introducing yourself to them, sharing something of yourself with them, seeing yourself through new eyes, seeing the world through their eyes. Existing within a collective—even for a short time—naturally dials up your curiosity and empathy. You ask questions, share thoughts, or simply share space. You're not a bystander, an observer, or a commentator. You're a contributor.

Get used to that feeling, and get used to finding new spaces and places to contribute. Get used being the newcomer, th beginner, to deciding which groups you want to join and which activities you want to contribute to. Notice how it feels, what you like or don't, where you feel the most confident or vulnerable.

Mostly, remember you're not alone. Everyone, all of us, are out here trying to find our way through this crazy world one permission at a time. Lowering the stakes and leveraging joy isn't feel-good frivolity; it's strategic; it's smart. Balance your maze of thoughts and feelings by making space for new life.

GETTING STARTED WITH SELF-PERMISSION

If you're ready to get started with self-permission—when you're ready—have a look at the website: www.tenpermissions.com/digital-workbook.com. There, you'll find a variety of resources to help you start to play around with permissions embed them into your life, and join others who are doing the same. You can download permission slips to write for yourself even if it feels corny because it will feel corny. Doesn't matter. It's a tangible action that will start to shift your lived reality. You can join a WhatsApp group with others walking similar paths as you.

However you want to move forward, there's help if you need it. Help to start to live a life that feels good and fits the moment.

You get to create that life.

You've got to.

ACKNOWLEDGMENTS

This book took over four years to write—four beautiful, challenging years to evolve, draft after draft, into what you've just read. So many people helped me along that long and winding path, keeping me going, directing and redirecting, urging me to rest when needed and to trust my voice. Chief among those was my husband, Christopher Rimmer, who watched me take my place at my computer screen year on year. Thank you for your patience and belief. Anneleigh Jacobsen, who got what was I trying to do early and never lost sight or stopped nudging me forward. Karin Schimke, you beauty! You came along at just the right time to bring this to completion. Jen Frahm, your inspiration, entertainment, and encouragement were like fuel along the way. Jacq Burns, for helping me to arrive at the shape and form of these *Ten Permissions*. Barb Durand-Brenner, the steadiest, gentlest set of hands. Members of the Explorers Group—and John Granholm and Anne Marie Rattray in particular—you've brought so much curiosity and kindness to me over the years.

ABOUT THE AUTHOR

JILLIAN REILLY is a founder, writer, public speaker, and consultant who spent her thirty-year career working in social, organizational, and individual change across Africa, Asia, and Central Europe.

Over the course of her career, she worked at both the grassroots and corporate levels, facilitating planning meetings under shady trees and in air-conditioned boardrooms, helping multinational charities design multimillion-dollar projects, and assisting community groups in planning their hundred-dollar budgets. In other words, she has just about "seen it all" in the aid industry.

Jillian's first book, *Shame: Confessions of an Aid Worker in Africa,* chronicles her early career in international aid and the hard lessons it taught her about making change. She has been published on international affairs in *The Washington Post*, *Newsweek*, and the *Los Angeles Times*. Jillian's TEDx talk, "Vain Aid," tells the story of her journey in the international aid industry and the lessons she's learned about changemaking along the way. Her *Courageous Conversations* podcast series, funded by the Ford Foundation, interviewed African activists and explored what it takes for them to continually show up and make change throughout their careers.